texting Olivia

Copyright © 2021 by GALYA GERSTMAN
All Rights Reserved.

ISBN 978-1-7364799-6-4
Library of Congress Control Number: 2021942072

Cover and Book Design by Lauren Grosskopf

*Pleasure Boat Studio books are available
through your favorite bookstore and through the following:*
Baker & Taylor, Ingram, Amazon, bn.com &
PLEASURE BOAT STUDIO: A NONPROFIT LITERARY PRESS
PLEASUREBOATSTUDIO.COM
Seattle, Washington

texting Olivia

by
GALYA GERSTMAN

Pleasure Boat Studio: A Nonprofit Literary Press

To My Mother

"Funny, you don't hear a single word I say.
…But the air you breathe I live to give you."

Brian May, "Father to Son"

Day One: **Arrival**

ME

We're here! Just got to the hotel. Come on over!

OLIVIA

Mom! It's finals!!! Remember??

ME

What? You're not coming?

OLIVIA

Fiiiiiinals mom!!!!

"She's not coming?" my husband, Neil, asked, shocked.

"Finals, she says."

"But Fay, we came all the way from New Jersey!" he squawked as he flopped onto the bed in our Marriott Court-yard room, tossing the throw pillows onto the beige upholstered chair in the corner. "I hate all these pillows," he grumbled. "I don't know why there's always so many goddamn pillows."

"I know," I agreed. "And why does everything have to always be beige? Hasn't any hotel decorator ever heard of teal or magenta?"

I looked over at Neil. Like myself, he's in his forties and graying. And also, like myself, he's of average weight, neither fat nor skinny, despite our love affair with Ben and Jerry's, though Neil appears slim because he is quite tall at six-foot-one, whereas I am only five-foot-six. Neil's eyes are green, and a bit wide apart, lending him a look of innocence that is belied by his smile, which turns up only on one side, as if he's smirking. As for me, I have a roundish face, lending me a somewhat youthful look that offsets my gray hair, and brown eyes that used to match my hair. Now they tend to match the dark circles beneath my eyes.

Neil's long frame lounged on the hotel bed, his feet hanging off. The framed prints above his head were of the Golden Gate Bridge. In case guests forgot where they were. In Miami hotels there were always prints of palm trees. I wondered if Alaskan hotels had photos of Kodiak bears.

Neil and I had traveled across the country to help our only child, Olivia, move out of her dorm, now that her freshman year was over, and bring all her copious belongings back home to New Jersey.

"So we have to wait till finals are over?!" Neil resumed his thread. "When do they end?"

"Wednesday," I told him.

"That's in two days, Fay! Are we not going to see her till Wednesday?!"

"She said maybe we can grab lunch or dinner together tomorrow."

"We came all the way out to San Francisco, and she'll see if she can fit us in?"

"Neil," I soothed him, "remember finals? Even you must have done some studying." Neil always vaunted how he had never studied nor gone to classes and still managed to get a BA. I sure was glad for once that our daughter never listened to him. But despite my defending her, in truth I, too, was put out.

ME
So we won't see you till tomorrow?

OLIVIA
Sorry mom. Finals!

OLIVIA
(adding)
But I'm so psyched you guys are here!!!

ME
So are we!!! But wish we could see you today...

OLIVIA
Gotta go back to studying

ME
OK. I understand. See you tomorrow then!

OLIVIA
For sure!

"So that's it? She's dumping us?" Neil complained.

"She's not dumping us, Neil. Try to be a little more understanding."

"No, that's your department, Fay," he countered. "You're the one who's always so understanding about whatever crap she pulls."

"Neil…"

"Remember the TB vaccine?" he prompted.

Before Olivia had even left for California, I had read the warnings on the university website that vaccine records were required in order to receive the first semester grades. So I contacted her pediatrician and obtained her records. But then a few weeks into the semester, I got a frantic call from her. Actually, any phone call from Olivia meant an emergency, since our default form of communication was now texting. After once calling her during class—I can't keep track of her school schedule—and another time at the hideously early hour of 10:00 a.m. on a Saturday, it was decided that it's safer to text her. Anyway, it seems she can't be bothered to pick up the phone anymore for anyone, even her cronies. It's all texting. "What did she say?" I'll ask her regarding a friend's response. "I don't know. She hasn't seen my text yet." "So call her!" "No, she'll see it soon." Thus, getting a phone call from Olivia meant serious business.

"Mom! They're telling me I can't get my grades because I haven't taken my TB vaccine!"

"What are you talking about?" I protested. "Of course you've gotten the TB vaccine! Remember when you started hyperventilating and the nurse had to have you lie down? And how she used a special baby needle for you?"

"I know!" she shrieked. "I told them! But they say they don't have a record of it!"

"What do you mean? It's there on the chart from Dr. Schlesinger!"

She didn't answer.

"Olivia, you still have the chart, right?"

"I can't remember where I put it."

"But didn't you submit it? They must have it in their files."

"Like I said, I don't remember where it is."

"But, again, did you not submit it?"

"No! Like I said, I can't find it!"

"She lost the chart?" Neil, who had overheard, asked in disbelief.

"Yeah," I grimaced. "Let me think what to do."

"What do you mean *let me think?*" he barked. "This is

her problem. And it's her fault she has this problem. So let her deal with it."

"Well, I don't know if she has Dr. Schlesinger's number."

"So send it to her, and let her call him," he said, leaning against our kitchen sink with the purple wall in the background. It had been Olivia's idea to paint the kitchen purple, and I love it because purple is my favorite color. Neil had groused about the color—*What's wrong with white?*—and about the mess and the fact that the kitchen was off-limits for two days, not to mention the paint fumes, which he was sure were giving us all cancer. But in the middle of the painting project Olivia had gotten invited to go to the beach with friends. So I ended up finishing the first wall and then decided it looked great with just that one wall painted as a pop of color. Plus I was tired.

"Okay," I agreed. "I'll send her his number." But afterwards I thought, *It's just so much easier for me to call the doctor and have him send it to me so I'll have it just in case something like this happens again.* I mean, sometimes you want the kid to learn a lesson, but other times you just want to take care of the matter. After all, we were talking about her getting her grades.

Neil claims I spoil Olivia. I don't really. I just want us to have a good relationship, unlike the one between my own mother and myself. Sometimes that means giving in a little bit and not complaining about every little thing. But there in our hotel room, I wasn't about to dip into this bowl of guacamole again, so I didn't answer. Anyway, it had been a long day and we were both tired. We had had to wake up at four to get to the airport, and then switch in Houston.

Thus, instead of heading into San Francisco proper, I suggested we pop over to the outdoor mall we'd spied on our way in, opposite our hotel, which was in a suburb. We spent the evening window shopping and ended up in PF Chang's for dinner. Yes, despite being in a city famous for its Chinatown, we dined in an ersatz Asian chain restaurant. We just wanted to make an early night of it. After all, we needed to recharge our batteries for all the fun we'd have the next day with our little girl!

This whole story started when Olivia told us she would have to evacuate her dorm at the end of the school year and bring all her stuff back home with her as well. And she had a lot of stuff.

"How is she going to bring all her crap?" Neil had asked me. Olivia had had to purchase at the outset a lot of the essentials—lamp, fan, mini-fridge, etc.—and then had spent the rest of the year acquiring "cool" things she found on the street or in the Salvation Army store.

"Good question. Maybe we'll have to go and help her?"

"Help her bring home a fridge?"

"Oh, she can sell that to someone, I'm sure," I had said, "or put it in storage. But as for all her clothing, we could put some in our suitcases."

"I told you not to buy her those boots for her birthday. At least you could have had them shipped here."

"But she wanted to wear them there," I had explained.

"So? You don't have to do everything she wants, Fay."

"Yeah, I didn't think."

"No," Neil had countered. "You just didn't want to refuse her. You never want to refuse her."

"Are we starting this again?"

"So now we have to go to San Francisco," he had griped, "and spend the money on plane tickets, a rental car, and a hotel. Great."

"Come on. It'll be fun."

"You know San Francisco is the most expensive city in the US?"

"So you've told me." Over and over.

We managed to purchase two round-trip tickets to San Francisco with the same return flight as Olivia's. We were very excited. She hadn't come home even for Christmas because she had been invited to spend the holidays with friends in L.A.

"Can't wait 2 c u," I had texted Olivia. No, I'm kidding. I can't stand incorrect grammar. After all, as a paralegal, I am used to documents which must be perfect. Put in an "and" instead of an "or" and it could cost the client thousands. And me my job. Olivia mocks me for always adding question marks and other punctuation she considers unnecessary and a flagrant waste of her valuable time. What I really texted was:

ME
Can't wait to see you!

OLIVIA
Can't wait 2 c u 2!!!

Ugh.

A week after we had purchased our tickets, Olivia texted me again about the move.

OLIVIA
Hey mom. Guess what? Me and Stephanie and Rachel are gonna move into an apartment together!

(Stephanie and Rachel were new friends she had made at college.)

ME
(confused)
I know. You already told us.

OLIVIA
No I mean now!!!!

ME
(even more confused)
Now? Not in the Fall?

OLIVIA
Now!!!!

ME
But you're not going to be there for the summer!
We're not going to pay rent for you to not be there!

OLIVIA
I'm going to get a friend to stay in my room and
pay Stephanie the rent

ME
But doesn't that mean that you will no longer
need us to come and bring all your stuff back
home?

No answer for a few moments, as she collected her thoughts, leaving me *on seen,* that is, she saw my text but didn't respond. Finally:

OLIVIA
But it will still be so great 2 c u!!!

ME

Yes, but we could have seen you here in NJ. I can imagine what your dad will say.

True to form, Neil had been apoplectic. *We already bought the plane tickets!* But I had assured him we were just as needed as before, only now we were going there to help her move from her dorm to her apartment. After all, she couldn't move all her possessions alone, as she herself had assured me. I also explained to him that Olivia said she was going to get a friend to sublet. Thus, the situation had been salvaged.

Two weeks later, in another exchange of texts, Olivia casually mentioned that she and her prospective roommates had rented a U-Haul.

ME

(My fingers flying over my phone's keyboard)
A U-Haul?! So again, you won't actually need us to move your stuff.

Again, radio silence on her part. Again, Neil had been beside himself. Again, I had calmed him down.

"We'll be going to help her pack," I had said, repeating Olivia's eventual save.

Honestly, none of these changes of plans had fazed me. I was okay with everything because I was just so happy to be seeing my girl again. And to bring her home.

Olivia had moved to San Francisco to study art. No one who had known Olivia since her teens would have been shocked by her career choice. My fairy princess of a little girl, who had evolved in adolescence into a sylphlike beauty with clear green eyes and long legs, a winning smile and perfect skin, with a cascade of honey-hued curls, gradually became bent on transforming herself into a walking art exhibit. Tattoos turned her limbs into a canvas for hieroglyphics, dyes lent her hair a palette of tones, and her face was studded with the titanium protuberances of piercings. Neil and my mother, Sophie, pester her about her "unnatural" look—Neil because of the foreign metals with which she has perforated her body and the toxic chemicals she slathers onto her scalp, Sophie because Olivia no longer looks like the girl she used to be, or the way she thinks a girl should look. Well, Neil probably thinks that too, though he is wise not to admit it. He focuses instead on the bane of his existence, harmful substances.

Neil is a bit of a hypochondriac, convinced the world around him is in league to contaminate him with some horrendous infection or disease. He alone has bumped up the stock market shares of the antibacterial gel industry. One of our favorite family anecdotes is about the time Neil started hyperventilating over a spot on his arm which he thought was melanoma. It turned out to be a spot of chocolate from the Snickers bar he had just snarfed. In any event, one of the consequences of my husband's hysteria is that he has turned into a pseudo health nut (because Snickers are still a food staple for him), starting the day with smoothies and supplements, and reading up on all the new superfoods. It takes him ten minutes just to swallow all his pills every morning.

Anyway, it was no surprise to any of us that Olivia wanted to study art. What was a surprise was where.

"California?" Neil and I had choked, as Olivia had announced her decision over dinner one night. Well, perhaps we had choked on the tofu lasagna I had made in Olivia's honor, since she had decided to become vegan. It wasn't one of my best efforts, to put it mildly. Luckily Neil had his private stash of ice cream sandwiches in the freezer, biding their time and keeping him calm.

"What's wrong with Rutgers?" Neil had asked.

"You're kidding, right?" Olivia had shot back. "Who studies art at Rutgers?"

"I assume they have an art department," I affirmed, as I grabbed the heavy, earthenware bowl of charred Brussels sprouts. Olivia had made the bowl in a ceramics class she'd attended the year before. It had a little lip on the edge which she confessed was actually accidental, but which I assured her fitted a serving spoon handle perfectly.

"Mom! If you want to study art, you go to art school!"

"But why in California?"

She eyed me with disdain. "Mom, New Jersey is not exactly the art mecca of the U.S."

"So what about New York?" Neil interjected. "You're not going to tell me New York is the sticks."

"Look," she sighed, making an effort to be patient with us. "New York is great, but I already know New York. I'm there every weekend. I need to expand my horizons. I need to experience new worlds."

"You sound like you're applying to NASA," I joked.

"I'm serious, guys. Don't you want me to be a success?"

"Of course we do, sweetie," I assured her. "But California? What about Boston, at least?"

"California is where the real art scene is," she assured us.

"I'm sorry but no. California is too expensive," Neil stated, exposing his biggest worry. Though he owned his own landscaping business, my husband always seemed to be fretting over funds. "And we'd have to pay out-of-state tuition."

"And it's so far," I added, exposing *my* biggest worry. "It's on the other side of the country. Of the continent. It's like you couldn't find a way to be farther away from us if you tried."

She looked out the big picture window facing our back yard, bordered by the curtains with little red cherries on them. I followed her gaze to the tree which, now that it was spring, sported fan-like pink blossoms. Olivia had planted it when she was a kid, and it was now taller than our house. I smiled inwardly at the irony that it was Olivia and not Neil who had planted it. Though Neil owns a landscaping company, he never did a thing with our back garden. The shoemaker's son always goes barefoot.

"So I'm never supposed to move away from home?" she screeched. "The farthest I can go is one state away? Don't you guys want me to become an adult? To spread my wings?" At this, she leaned back in the black faux leather chair and spread her arms out. The window in front of which she was sitting was curtained with the same cherry pattern. Through it one could see the thick hedges separating our yard from that of our neighbors, the Perettis. Their three children had left home years ago. I would sometimes see the older couple on their morning walks. They walked together, and always waved at me as I pulled out of our driveway on my way to work. They seemed happy.

"If you wanted to become an adult," Neil said, "you'd get a job."

"I don't want a *job*," Olivia spat, making the word sound like an infection. "I want a career."

"Oh, and being an artist is having a career? How's that going to put food on the table?" he challenged.

"Not again with this!" she cried. "All you ever think about is making money!"

"Well, if I didn't think about making money, we wouldn't even be having this conversation!" he yelled back. "If I didn't make a decent living, you'd be lucky to even go to college!"

"Okay, okay, this is getting us nowhere," I cut in, trying to soothe tempers. "We can't impose upon Olivia our choice of profession," I said to Neil.

"That's right, Dad," Olivia chimed in, vindicated. "You guys got to choose what you wanted to do. Now I get to choose what I want to do."

I didn't actually get to choose what I wanted to do, I thought. I had wanted to be a lawyer but my mother, who by then was a widow, had balked at the idea of law school. It would cost too much money, she had said. It would take too long, she had said. I would have to drop out in the middle once I got married and had kids, she had said. So I became a paralegal instead. I work for a lawyer in a small office that was once someone's house, just a fifteen-minute drive from our home in Piscataway.

"But I'd only see you, like, twice a year if you moved to California," I pouted. My meal was getting cold and I was losing my appetite.

"We'd still Skype," she promised, turning back to me, "and see each other on vacations."

In the end we agreed to let Olivia at least apply to schools in California, along with New York and New Jersey.

But it wasn't as easy as she had expected. First, she had to take the SATs. As her first go produced rather dismal results, I enrolled her in an SAT-prep course, which was being offered Saturdays in a nearby high school. She had been going for several weeks when I happened to pass by the school. It was, as these institutions are wont to be, an uninspired and, I am sure, uninspiring square and squat concrete monstrosity that only needed some barbed wire and a tower to resemble a prison. As I was turning around the corner, lo and behold I spied my daughter and two other kids outside, leaning against the side of the building and smoking cigarettes. Now, I knew she smoked, though Neil didn't. He would have had a fit, but I remembered myself at her age sneaking cigarettes in the park down the street from my house, so I kept mum. When I returned from my errand the same way, however, Olivia and company were still outside smoking. I thus made a U-turn and pulled up alongside the group, whereupon the other two scattered. Olivia waved and then made as if to go back with them but I called her over through my open window.

"Hi Mom," she said casually.

"Hi yourself. What are you doing outside?"

"I was just taking a little break."

"A little break? Olivia, I passed by here fifteen minutes ago, and you were outside. How long of a break do you usually take?"

"Well, I guess I went in and then came back out."

"You guess? So you come out every fifteen minutes?"

"I don't know. I wasn't timing it or anything."

"Olivia, you *are* going to the classes, aren't you?"

"'Course I am!"

"Because these classes aren't cheap, and you really need to do well on your SATs this time."

"I know, I know! It's just that it's so boring!" she remarked, drawing out the word "boring."

"Olivia! You begged me to enroll you in this course!" I reminded her.

"I know!"

"It's costing hundreds of dollars!" I couldn't help but add.

"I know!"

"And it's for your benefit, not ours, you know."

"I know, Mom! I'm going in now. See?" She turned to go, pirouetting and flashing me a smile.

I knew my face wore a worried look but I tried to be relaxed.

"Bye," I said, waving my fingers.

"Bye," she answered as she opened the side door to the building, and then suddenly leapt back out again, pretending to escape. Her grin was a mile wide.

"Ha ha," I said, but I did laugh. That Olivia.

In the end, her SAT grades improved a bit, enough, apparently, to get into the school of her choice. Which I suppose was due to her portfolio. That had been another palaver.

"How do I make a portfolio?" she'd asked me.

"I don't know," I'd replied honestly. I knew from CVs but not from portfolios. Neil was no help either. So it was up to me to help her. We looked up "portfolios" online. We consulted with her art teacher. We asked a friend who had studied fashion design. And then basically we rounded up Olivia's best paintings and art projects, photographed them and uploaded them all onto the school's website application.

Olivia received three letters of acceptance, one of course from California. The school cited her outstanding portfolio, lauding it especially for its magnitude. Indeed, she was accepted there with a half-scholarship, which mollified Neil a bit, and finally made us cave in to her desire. She was going to California.

Even worse, I wasn't the one who ended up accompanying her there, but rather my younger brother did. Gabe, whose wavy brown hair is just beginning to gray at the temples, is two years my junior. He is a lawyer, married, and has two kids still in their early teens, Brian and Erin. He works for a huge corporation headquartered in Germany, and happened to have business in San Francisco exactly when Olivia was meant to go. It was just reasonable and practical, therefore, not to mention economical, for my brother to meet her and take her to her school and her dorm. So I had to say goodbye to Olivia in Newark Airport. I was already pining away for her before she even left.

Olivia and I have a wonderful relationship. You couldn't ask for a better daughter. She has always been warm and loving, full of excitement, enthusiasm and joy. Like a hummingbird, Olivia would whiz around at the speed of light, blinding me so that I could hardly keep up. But when she'd stop for a rare second, she'd shine, and shower me with love and attention. Even as a small child, when I would tuck her in every night, she would tell me how much she loved me. Over the months and years her parameters of affection grew and grew.

"I love you," I'd say, pulling the covers up to her chin.

"I love you more," she'd counter.

"You can't love me more," I'd explain facetiously. "Because moms love the most."

Aha. A dare. Olivia couldn't resist a dare. "But I love you more than…the sky."

Later: "I love you more than the universe."

It progressed to: "I love you more than God."

Finally, one day, "I love you more than my own life."

With Olivia, it always had to be more.

But to be perfectly honest, Olivia hadn't been an easy child. As a baby, still in the womb, she had tossed and turned so much that she got the umbilical cord wrapped around her neck. This was why she didn't descend into the vaginal cavity, according to the obstetrician, and why I had to have a C-section. As a newborn she cried and cried. Neil and I didn't know what was wrong with her. Colic? Diaper rash? Something serious? *Why won't she stop that wailing?* We spent days and nights holding her, rocking her, walking the house with her, and eventually handing her off to one of her grandmothers. It was exhausting. She was exhausting. Olivia would later be diagnosed with Attention Deficit Hyperactivity Disorder, or ADHD—well, duh, she couldn't sit quietly even in the womb. A stranger passing by would have been able to diagnose her. She would fuss as a baby, fidget as a child, whine as a teen. She would grow bored quickly and would always want to be elsewhere. If we were home, Olivia wanted to be out; if we were eating Italian she wanted Chinese; if it was summer she wished it were winter. The novelty of everything wore off rapidly, and she would literally sob from boredom. It was debilitating.

As a result, Olivia always needed something new, something fresh; she was constantly pushing boundaries. Like the time she told me she had a crush on a boy in her high school.

"That's so great," I said. "What's his name?"

"It's Colin."

"Good name."

"Well, now it's Colin."

"What do you mean, now?"

"Well, he's a tran. He used to be a girl."

"Oh, I see," I sputtered. "Okay. Okay. So..." I scrambled for something to say to appear nonchalant. "What was his name before? Colleen?"

"Yes! How did you guess?"

"Oh, I don't know. Just lucky."

"So, you don't think it's weird, do you?"

"Um, weird? Um, no! No, it's not weird. Live and let live, I say."

"I knew you'd understand. You're so cool, Mom."

And there you have it, my fatal flaw: I gave in to peer

pressure. I wanted to be cool. I wanted her to like me. So I'd sacrifice my true thoughts and feelings, bottle them up, and pretend to be cool. And honestly, I wanted to be cool. I didn't want to be intolerant of trans people. I wanted to think it was okay. I mean, I did think it was okay. I just felt...weird. I just imagined my daughter with a girl-turned-guy and I hesitated. But that's okay, isn't it? At least I was trying. Cut me some slack—I was born in the seventies. This was all new to me. When she would tell me that one of her peers had just come out to the class, I was always shocked and impressed that we as a species had come so far. In my time, you couldn't even admit you went to dance classes if you were a high school boy, or that you could fix a car if you were a girl. Guys couldn't even wear purple without getting beat up after school. In the end I forced myself to imagine Olivia kissing another woman and realized I could be fine with it. I'd be happy with whoever could make her happy. *Good luck to them, ha ha!* I thought. *Just try and keep up.* As it happened, Colin decided he wasn't into her. She cried to me. "Even guys who used to be girls don't find me attractive!"

She still cries to me from California about one thing or another. If it isn't about her friends, it's about boys. What did Scott mean when he said he had had a good time? Why hadn't he said he'd had a great time? Or else it was about her work load. She couldn't cope, it was too much. Everyone finished their work on time except her. She was incompetent. Or if it wasn't about the quantity of work, it was about its quality. She wasn't good enough, creative enough, driven enough. *Artists,* I sighed to myself. *So sensitive.* And what could I do, since she was over there in San Francisco, California and I was over here in Piscataway, New Jersey? Still, if you can't cry to your mom, whom *can* you cry to?

Well, I didn't cry to my mom when I was a teen, because we didn't have that kind of relationship. Sophie was a good mom, I guess; I mean, she put food on the table and clothes on our backs, but she was not a particularly sensitive mother. Whenever I would voice doubts or fears as a child or teen, she'd chide me not to be so silly or so stupid, in those words exactly and in a tone of disregard or outright scorn. She didn't see it as being mean; she simply thought or rather knew that my problems were insignificant. They were not real problems like poverty or war, both of which she had suffered. My problems were comfy, middle-class tribulations: my hair was frizzy, I missed my show on TV, and the like.

Olivia's difficulties were similarly benign to my weathered worldview, but to her they were dire enough to bring her to tears. I never dismissed them—I never dismissed her—and I never added insult to injury by telling her she was stupid to feel so horrible. Instead I tried to share her sorrow, as if I could absorb her pain and thus lessen it, and sometimes it seemed I could. Sometimes it seemed by taking on her sadness I was lightening her load. Sometimes I even had words of wisdom to help her plow through. I always prided myself on at least trying my best to alleviate her worries, unlike my own mother for me, and to field with an open mind whatever she would throw at me.

OLIVIA
Guess what mom? I did a photo shoot!

ME
A photo shoot? Like for a magazine?

OLIVIA
No it's this guy who's a freelance photographer

and he does these arty photos that he posts on his blog

ME
Cool! Can I see them?

OLIVIA
(pause)
Um I'm not so sure you'd like them

ME
(Ding! Ding! Alarms are ringing.)
Why not? What kind of photos are they?
They're not nude photos, are they?
(Bile is rising up my throat.)

OLIVIA
No. Not nude
(phew!)

ME
So?

OLIVIA
Well he gave me these costumes. They were really pretty. Lots of gauze
(pause again)

ME
And?

OLIVIA
Um you might find them a bit skimpy. Like you can see my bra and underwear

ME

Your bra and underwear show through the
costumes?

OLIVIA

They sort of are the costumes, with this delicate
fabric swirled around me

ME

Oh my God, Livy, is this guy legit? Are these
photos going to appear all over the internet?

OLIVIA

No he has this blog but he said he wouldn't use
any photos without my permission

ME

Oh, he said that. Did you sign anything?
Did he sign anything?

OLIVIA

Mom he's a good friend of Stephanie's! And he's
an artist. Anyway it was a completely different
type of shoot

ME

Different how?
(She doesn't answer. Shit.)

ME

How exactly were you posed, Olivia?

OLIVIA

Well I was sort of...tied up

ME

What?!

OLIVIA

But not in a weird way! It was very artistic!

She finally agreed to send me some photos, and I quake to think what the other photos looked like if these were the presentable ones. It looked like she was in a harem in hell. *If anyone ever sees them!* I thought, and made her promise never to do anything like that again without talking to me first. But, of course, the next time it will be something else, something completely different but similarly obscene or insane, which Olivia will think sounds like a good idea. And which I will have to hide from my mother.

It's not that I am scared of my mother, exactly. She's this tiny thing, five-foot-two, and is now seventy years old. She is slim, always perfectly coiffed and dressed to the nines, sparing no amount of sparkle. She has a host of friends. Everyone loves her. As do I, of course. I mean, she's my mom. Everyone loves their mom, right? It's just that Sophie's world-view is so different from mine, and anything unorthodox or imaginative is met with her suspicion or disapproval, which she is never afraid to share. She is moreover unbending in her conviction that she's right and everyone else is wrong, no matter the subject. In a different way than my daughter, she, too, is exhausting.

This is why I asked Olivia to do me a favor, a small favor with regard to her grandmother, in preparation for her return from San Francisco with us.

OLIVIA

"What?"

I swear I could read her defensiveness there already. From the age of thirteen, Olivia met all my requests with suspicion, as if I had an ulterior motive. She was well aware any mention of my mother was always fraught with tension for me. My relationship with my mother has always been...complicated. To Olivia, Grandma Sophie is a loving, spirited, feisty old lady whom she doesn't take all too seriously. To me, my mother is indeed loving but oppressive, spirited but judgmental, feisty but critical. And God forbid I should call her old.

Frankly, in my forties, I was the one who was old, that is, too old to be cowering before my mother on any account. It's not that I'm such a wuss; it's that she's such a harpy sometimes, and I'm too tired to stand up for my principles anymore. Hmm, I guess that is getting old. Or maybe it's because I am surrounded by arguments all day, being a paralegal. Sometimes I just feel like telling our clients to shut the fuck up and stop fighting. One of my boss's specialties is divorce law and we both joke that seeing the hassle and pettiness of our clients' brawls, not to mention the reams of paperwork and days of wasted time in court appearances, are enough to guarantee we'll never leave our husbands, even if they were serial killers.

I told Olivia what I wanted. "Hide your nose piercing from Grandma." My daughter had recently decided to add an Elsie-the-cow ring to go with her other piercings, tattoos and not-found-in-nature hair colors. I myself don't mind the hair color rainbow so much because I know eventually it will grow out (or fall out, most likely), and even the piercings don't keep me up nights because they can be removed. The tongue piercing did get infected, though, causing her tongue to balloon so that she couldn't eat for days. She had to finally remove it, but did that daunt her? No. She went back and had an even bigger one reinserted once she had recovered.

It's the tattoos that really get to me. I know, I know, everyone has a tattoo nowadays. I'm not against all tattoos. If she only had a little one on her shoulder, or behind her neck, or even what they call a *tramp stamp* down toward the backside, I could find it acceptable, or at least bearable. But that would be boring, in her view. She had to get gargantuan ones, along her entire arms. You can practically see them from space. Now she has started talking about expanding to her legs.

"No, not the legs, Olivia!" I begged. She has long, slim, model's legs, ideally proportioned between thigh and lower leg. They are flawless. It would be like spray-painting graffiti on the Venus de Milo, or pasting bumper stickers on a Jaguar.

Olivia is wounded by our opposition to her self-embellishments. Couldn't we understand this is her way of expressing herself? If I even hint at my disapproval, she won't talk to me for days. I hate to hurt her feelings so eventually I learned to just shut up, most of the time. But now that she was returning to New Jersey, now that we were going to see my mother, I needed Olivia to hide the latest, and most egregiously in-your-face, literally, piercing she had just gotten. I knew it could be done. I'd seen her do it. She'd hidden the thing when she video-called me for my birthday (because even my teenage daughter wouldn't be so callous as to text me birthday greetings) by turning it up inside her nose to fool me into thinking she'd finally removed it. Getting my hopes up only to dash them, ha ha.

Olivia now asked me why she needed to hide her nose-ring.

ME

Why do you think? Because Grandma will blame it on me, of course. She'll say I'm a bad mother for letting you do it.

OLIVIA

Letting me do it???? Why would she think you or anyone else would have that power over me?

(Because she has that power over me, I didn't say.)

OLIVIA

But do you think you're a bad mother?

ME

Honestly? No.

(Although according to my mother...)
Well, maybe sometimes.

OLIVIA

Why? I think you're a great mom

ME

Aww, thanks.

But maybe that's because I'm such a soft touch, I thought. Parents are supposed to be parents, not friends, according to Neil; limit-imposers, like my mother, not coddlers or put-up-with-everythingers. Like me.

My mother certainly would not have let me get away with not coming to see her if she had flown all the way out to San Francisco. My mother never put up with anything. If I got anything less than a B in school, she grounded me for a month. Once, when I was a teen, she warned me to pick my clothes up from the floor. I answered that it was my room and it didn't bother me. When I returned home from school that day, I found she had thrown out my dirty socks, underwear, jeans and T-shirt. I had to sneak out to the garbage can to retrieve them. That sure taught me a lesson. All my friends were afraid of Sophie. As was I, then. Now, well, I'm not really afraid of her, per se. I just sometimes don't want to have to deal with her. With her, it's always something. If my mother can't find anything to complain about, she'll just make something up.

Exhibit A: Preet. Preet is the physical therapist I hired to visit my mother twice a week after she injured her rotator cuff. We all adore him, except for my mother, who is convinced he is robbing her blind.

"It's making me sick!" she exclaimed during one of my visits. "Sick, I tell you! *Sickkke!*"

"Why would Preet steal your sweaters?" I asked. Her sweater collection rivals Imelda Marcos's infamous shoe hoard. She is always cold so she has an apartment full of sweaters. She even has summer sweaters, in case of a rebel breeze. All of them are black.

"He's from Nepal, you know," she answered, rolling her eyes at my stupidity. "It's cold there."

"But Mom, your sweaters are size small. He's, like, five-foot-ten."

"Did I say it was for him? He has a family, you know."

And it's not just the sweaters. The guy will steal anything, apparently.

"Your polyester pants? With the elastic waist? Why on earth would he steal those?"

"What are you saying? What's wrong with my pants? You know how much those pants cost me?"

"How much?" I called her bluff.

"Well, I got them on sale, as it so happens, but originally they were very expensive."

She gets everything on sale. Unlike my late father, who to her dismay was always outrageously liberal with his cash, she would rather die than pay full price for anything.

As for the thieving Preet, she must have believed he was also stealing food from her because Gabe, during one of his visits, found a bag of rice in my father's old sock drawer. He chalked it up to our mother's squirrel mentality, since she stocks up on dried and canned goods as if she's expecting an invasion from Mars, but I knew it was because she was hiding it from Preet. After all, the last cleaning woman quit because she claimed my mother was counting the bananas.

"The bananas, Mom?" I had scolded, exasperated. "Really?"

"I wasn't counting them," she had protested. "It's just, I mean, how many bananas could the woman eat? There'd be a whole bunch when I went to bed and when I woke up, there would be only three!"

"So you *were* counting them!"

"I was not! It was just so obvious! Who wouldn't notice a whole bunch turning into three overnight? Hmm?"

Gabe and I tried to make her consider the possibility—a small, minuscule possibility, perhaps—that these people weren't stealing from her but rather that she was getting confused and forgetting where she had put things.

"That's what you think of me?" she thundered. "You think I'm crazy? You think I'm senile?"

"We're not saying that, Mom," I began, trying to defuse the situation.

"You believe that…that…hoodlum over me?" she asked, incredulous and offended.

"That's not what we're saying…"

"Yes, that's what you're saying! I'm not stupid. And I'm not crazy!"

"Mom…"

"Get out. The both of you!" Whereupon she threw us out of her apartment. We had to grovel the next day and apologize. It's a maddeningly fine line we tread trying to placate her without contesting her sanity nor confirming Preet's guilt. But since Gabe lives so far away, it's generally up to me to sort things out with my mother.

As a result, I am usually the one on the receiving end of my mother's craziness. Exhibit B: Sophie has been on a diet since the invention of the scale, or at least as far as anyone can remember. She weighs herself twice a day—yes, twice a day—and if she sees she's gained half a pound, she stops eating dinner for a few days, replacing it with a piece of fruit. Recently, she told me her breakfast consisted of a cup of coffee with five saltine crackers. Now, I know she's not out running marathons at her age, and I'm no nutritionist, but five crackers seem somewhat on the paltry side as far as the day's most important meal goes. This caloric self-restraint has always driven me crazy. She's seventy! At her age, even her doctors tell her that the goal is to remain healthy, not lose weight. But does she listen? In fact, she lost so much weight over a few months that my brother wanted me to take her for tests.

"You know sudden weight loss is a cancer symptom," he fretted. Gabe has inherited my mother's worry gene, and is often convinced her house will explode or she will get a stroke or an axe-murderer will visit her in the night.

"You don't get it, Gabe," I tried to explain. "She does it *on purpose*. She is actively trying to lose weight. She skips dinner for days if she's gained a few ounces."

One can thus imagine what growing up with her was like. Even now she'll admonish me over my food choices.

"You don't need that croissant," she said to me one Sunday when Neil, Olivia and I had taken her out for brunch.

"Um, yes, I realize I don't *need* it. I *want* it. What's the big deal?"

"I just mean you should watch what you eat, that's all. You don't want to ruin all your hard work."

Where do I start? I did not *work hard* to lose any weight. That's her mindset, not mine. I might be carrying around a few too many pounds, but nothing outrageous. Moreover, I refuse to live as she has, as a sentinel on the lookout forever for any stray calories that would dare try to breach her fortress.

She won't give up, however. "Don't be insulted, but…"

Now, you know when you hear that preamble, your

insult neurons start firing away in your brain. *Red alert! Repeat: Red alert! This is not a drill! Prepare to engage!* "Don't be insulted, but I think you might have taken on a few pounds." Taken on, like stowaway travelers. I don't answer, so she pursues. "Not too much, just a bit. You just need to take care, to watch what you eat."

Sometimes we begin to bicker. Sometimes my own insecurities convince me she is right—though we still bicker. When has one's mother being right ever stopped anyone from arguing with her?

Sophie manages to raise the ugly diet red flag even when she can't see me. She doesn't know how to use video-calling no matter how many times my brother and I have taught her. We bought her an iPad for that purpose but she kept forgetting to charge it, and even when it was charged she'd forget which icon to press.

"So, how's the diet going?" she'll infallibly ask when she calls. I have long ceased to pick a fight with her about this. She always assumes that, like herself, my life has been one long battle with baked goods.

"Fine, fine," I assure her.

"Are you watching?"

Not the Oscars; my food intake.

"I'm fine, Mom, really."

"Good. I'm glad to hear it. You know what it's like. So quick to gain and then it's so hard to lose. Who knows better than me?"

I let her think I agree with her—basically hiding again, by feigning acquiescence—all the while scoffing at her in my head. And scoffing at her to Olivia. I don't worry about my own daughter's body perception and how all this talk of dieting might be affecting her, since Olivia has always been naturally thin, what with her whirling dervish metabolism.

My mother's dieting, finally, is just one facet of a larger

theme, Sophie's all-encompassing obsession with her looks. My mother is the spokesperson for vanity, its *grande dame*, its poster child. She dyes her hair, won't wear her glasses, and refuses to even consider a cane. She practically puts lipstick on to go to the toilet. When she sprays on perfume, I swear she opens a little gash in the ozone layer. I have to struggle for breath. Even her apartment is done up like a French whore, furnished in Louis XIV or baroque furniture. All I know is she never met a tassel she didn't like, and if it's gold, all the better. There isn't a straight line in her place; it's all curlicues and spirals. The drapes are red velvet, if that tells you anything.

A while ago, Sophie asked me to accompany her to the mall—because a woman who can't see without glasses and doesn't use a cane can't risk walking unaccompanied—to buy a new moisturizer, one with retinol, for preventing wrinkles.

"I've started to see some lines around my mouth," she confided, in all seriousness. Well, thank God she doesn't wear her glasses, because it's afforded her the illusion that only recently, at the age of seventy, she has begun to wrinkle. Still, she's made some concessions to old age: she will wear her glasses at least while she drives, and because her eyesight isn't what it used to be, she only drives short distances, like to the neighborhood supermarket, and no longer at night. She has also started wearing shoes with shorter heels, and has only accepted a hearing aid because now they make them small and unobtrusive. Before, she would balk: "But people will think I'm old!" only half-jokingly. Anyway she almost never wears it because it is either out of batteries, its battery is being charged, or she doesn't want to waste the battery… by actually using it.

She can't hear me when I'm sitting right next to her, but somehow, over the phone, miles away, even through a bad connection, I only have to open my mouth and say,

"Hi, Mom," and she'll ask, "Do you have a cold?" How it is that she can hear the slight hoarseness in my voice, or a barely-there wheeze, I can't fathom. Similarly, she has super powers of smell, as she would demonstrate when I was a teenager. I would come home at night, hardly through the front door, and she would sniff, "Have you been smoking?"

To my shock, Olivia recently claimed I was the apple who had fallen from my mother's tree. After I had filled her in on my usual Sophie complaints, she texted:

OLIVIA
But you're just as bad as she is!!!!
(laughing emoji)

ME
What are you talking about?

OLIVIA
Like u won't wear ur glasses in public

ME
(forced to accede)
OK yes, but then again, I am not legally blind without them.

OLIVIA
Um u'll say hello to total strangers and snub close friends so long as u don't look unattractive

She was right, of course. I told her about my trip to the dermatologist, worried about a new mole. (Actually, Neil had been worried.) As part of the full-body checkup, the doctor had to look at my scalp, which meant she had to riffle through my still wet hair. I'd end up looking like a fluffy dandelion. *Oh no!* I realized. *I'm meeting Elaine for lunch! How can I let her see me like that?!* I actually entertained the idea of asking the doctor to skip the scalp, when I stopped myself. *You would prefer to let possible melanoma go unchecked and kill you rather than have your friend see you with frizzy hair?* I asked myself. *How vain are you?*

When I related this to Olivia, she texted another laughing emoji.

OLIVIA
Ha ha. C? U r turning into Grandma!

This was a blow below the belt. But two could play at this game...

ME
Yeah, ha ha. I guess I'm becoming like Grandma. But guess what? So are you.

OLIVIA
Me????
(I could practically see her choking.)

ME
Yes, you.

OLIVIA
No way!!!!

ME
Yes, way. I refer you to your love of jewelry, and indeed all things sparkly.

OLIVIA
(typing)
I don't

ME
(cutting her off)
When's the last time you bought yourself jewelry?

OLIVIA
U mean real

ME
(again cutting her off)
No, don't use that cop-out. I know you're not
out shopping at Harry Winston. But when's
the last time you bought a ring or earrings or
something?

OLIVIA
Uh...yesterday
(She's cringing, I'm sure.)

Olivia has followed in the tiny footsteps of my mother, who is so overflowing with jewelry that she started giving stuff to me and Olivia because she simply hasn't got the room or the appendages for it all. On all other matters my mother is quite the skinflint, but that is one of the few areas her stinginess doesn't touch. When it comes to baubles she is convinced, like the old L'Oreal commercial, she's worth it. Olivia, too, can't resist the bling, albeit in its shabby chic version of stuff from street fairs and second-hand shops.

ME
Oh, there's another way you're like her!

(I crowed)
Thrift stores! You both love thrift stores!

To be fair, Olivia's love of thrift shops stems from their being eco-friendly, offering one-of-a-kind fashion (as opposed to two people wearing the same Zara dress to a party—I've seen it happen) and, well, because they're hip. When she introduced Sophie to her favorite second-hand store in New Jersey, my mother was in heaven.

"Look at this! Will you just look at thissss?" she brayed. Sophie has a way of pronouncing things, of putting the stress on the last consonants, which Olivia loves to imitate, to really emphasize the word. *Thissss.* "It's ten dollars! Can you imagine?"

"Cool, Grandma!"

"And I bet if I work my magic, I can get them to lower it even more."

Olivia gaped at her in horror. "Oh my God, Grandma, please don't." She turned to me, her look pleading. She probably shopped there all the time. She would never be able to show her face again.

"Mom, you're going to haggle over a ten-dollar sweater?" I began. I don't know why I thought insinuating she was cheap would work. On the contrary, she takes pride in it.

"What do you think?" she parried. "Your father didn't work hard for his money, that I should just throw it away?"

My father had been a lawyer, and had left us in a relatively decent financial state, though my mother had gotten a job as a bank teller, eventually, worried our nest egg would run out. She had for as long as I remember always held on to her purse strings with an iron fist.

"Ten dollars is not throwing away money, Mom."

"Just mind your own business and let me talk."

While she approached the cash register, we hot-footed it out the door.

I continued musing to Olivia about her and my mother.

ME

Hmm, let me see, what else? You both love black!

OLIVIA

Give me a break mom. Everyone loves black

ME

No, not everyone.

OLIVIA

Oh right. Not everyone ha ha

Meaning me. For both Olivia and my mother only black is acceptable to wear, Olivia on account of its being arty and Sophie because it's slimming. My mother's closet looks like the antechamber to a funeral parlor, and my daughter's to an Ozzie Osbourne concert. They look at me with amusement and/or revulsion whenever I wear my purple paisley pants.

OLIVIA

**I need sunglasses just to go into your closet.
The anti-glare kind!!**

ME

At least I don't wear black lipstick.

OLIVIA

What's wrong with black lipstick

ME

Nothing, Morticia.

OLIVIA

Ha ha

ME

Been on a lot of dates, lately?

OLIVIA

Not funny mom

ME
(Oh no. I had hurt her feelings!)
Kidding!

But she had hurt mine. Was I really turning into my mother?

One day a few years ago, Olivia was screeching out a song, and I stopped cold when I heard the lyrics.

"Olivia, what the hell are you singing?"

"It's just a song, Mom."

"*We fuck for life?* That's a song?"

"Oh Mom," she sneered. "You sound just like Grandma Sophie."

I remember when my mother would hear me playing Bruce Springsteen, New Jersey's favorite son (up until Bon Jovi arrived).

"You call that a voice?" Sophie carped. "That's not a voice. Now, Frank Sinatra, that's a voice."

"It's not his voice that's important, Mom," I'd counter. "It's the songs he writes."

"How can you even understand them? I can't even understand the words!"

Well, I can understand the words to Olivia's choice of songs, but I can't believe them. The other day I heard a song on the radio in which the singer sang, "I want to fuck you like an animal." What?! When I was growing up, Peter Frampton's "I'm In You" was banned in Boston. And it wasn't even meant literally.

Once, when I was little, maybe eight or nine, I had gotten a solo part in our school music festival. My parents were oh so proud. I remember my mother fussing over my dress, a red and white gingham monstrosity, and pulling my hair back into so severe a ponytail that I could barely blink my eyes, my skin was so taut. She kept reminding me to sing loudly and clearly, so that even those in the back of the auditorium would be able to hear. I was nervous enough having to stand alone and sing in front of such a crowd; I didn't need her ramping up the tension. Anyway, I managed to pull it off, and my parents even recorded it on tape with a new tape recorder they had bought just for the occasion.

A few weeks later, my mother's sister and brother-in-law, Aunt Deirdre and Uncle Leo, came to visit. On their second evening together, my mother suddenly got the idea of playing for Deirdre and Leo the recording of my moment of glory.

"Fay," my mother called to me, for I was upstairs in my room, "bring down the tape recorder. We want to play for your aunt and uncle how you sang in the music festival."

Upstairs, I froze.

"Okayyy," I called down, my thoughts and heart racing. *Oh no! They can't hear that tape!*

After my parents had replayed my singing the evening of the festival, I became intrigued with the machine.

Wow! A machine that recorded stuff. A machine that could record anything you said into it. I invited my best friend, Karen, over to see it.

"Imagine what you could do with a machine like that,"

we mused aloud. "Just imagine."

"Turn it on," Karen said. I showed her how you had to press the play and record buttons at the same time. We began giggling, nervous.

"Say something," I commanded Karen.

"Like…wwhat?" she stuttered.

"Anything," I said.

"Anything?"

"Yeah. I dare you."

"Fay!" my mother yelled. "I said bring the tape recorder!"

"I'm coming!" I squeaked, sweat oozing down my neck. *No no no! What do I do?* "Hey Mom! I got a better idea! I can sing the song for them in person!"

"No, it won't be as good without the music! Bring it down, I said!"

"Yes! It will!" I started down the stairs. My mother was standing at the bottom, hands on her hips.

"Fay," she lowered her voice, which was even more menacing than her yells. "I won't tell you again. Bring. It. Down. Right. Now."

So like a convict taking his last walk along the Green Mile to the gallows, I picked up the vehicle of my doom and slowly descended the stairs towards the kitchen, where all were gathered around the table.

"Wait'll you hear this," my mother bragged.

"It's so cute!" my father beamed. And this is what they heard:

"…O beautiful, for spacious skies, for amber waves of— (static, hiss)(giggles) Shit." (More giggles)

"Son of a bitch." (Goofier giggles)

"Damn!" (Laughs more raucous now)

My parents were silent, their faces slowly turning red.

"Whore!" (Whooping laughs on the tape)

"Fuck!" (Guffaws)

"Mother fucker!!"

Click. My mother's finger on the stop button. Her breathing belabored. She had been particularly scandalized by "mother fucker," taking it literally, I suspect, when all it had meant to Karen and me was a really, really dirty thing to say.

My mother marched me up to my bedroom, then and there. I knew I wasn't going to get away with just having my mouth washed out with soap, which is what she had done on the occasions I let slip a bad word in her presence. I had thought the bitter bar of soap being shoved down my gullet was bad. But I knew now, having compounded my guilt by spewing multiple curse words, by having inadvertently erased my taped performance, and by shaming my mother in front of her sister and brother-in-law, that I could expect nothing less than the thrashing of my life, using her old standby, the trusty wooden spoon. This time she didn't even bother with the lame preamble that it would hurt her more than it hurt me. Shaking with uncontrolled fury, she wanted it to hurt. Even when my father called outside my bedroom door, which she had locked, that that was enough already, she kept hitting me. I couldn't sit for days afterwards.

No, I am not just like Grandma Sophie.

Day **Two**

ME

Hi! When do we meet up?

ME

Hi again! When do we meet up?

ME

Why aren't you answering your phone or texts??

Our texts went unanswered for most of the morning, and our phone calls were answered with, "The number you have reached…" Finally, after 1:00 p.m.—1:00 p.m.!—Olivia sent me a text.

OLIVIA

OMG mom!!! So so sorrrrrryyyyy!!!! I was up the whole night and didn't get to bed til 6!!!

ME

I was wondering why you didn't answer!

OLIVIA

I just slept through your calls, I was so tired!!

ME

Never mind. Feeling hungry?

OLIVIA

Mom you're going to kill me but I still haven't finished my final project!! It's due tomorrow!!!

ME

So? You still have to eat!

OLIVIA

I'm just going to grab a yogurt and try and finish this!

ME

Are you kidding?

OLIVIA

Mom please don't put pressure on me!!! I'm already freaking out that I won't get it done on time!!!

ME

Why did you leave it for the last minute???

OLIVIA

The last minute??? I've been working on it for two daaaayyyys!! Thx for the vote of confidence!!

ME

OK sorry. So what about meeting for dinner?

OLIVIA

I hope so but it depends on if I finish or not

ME

Oh I see.

OLIVIA

(Correctly reading my tone.)
Don't be like that mom!!!! Don't you think I
would rather go out with you guys???

ME

It's just that we came all the way from NJ.

OLIVIA

I know! I'm soooo sorrrrryyy!!! I'll really try to
finish by tonight!!

ME

OK. Just want to see you!

OLIVIA

Me 2! And I bought u all presents!

ME

Aw, you didn't have to!

"She bought us presents, Neil! She's just so sweet!" I
called out to Neil who was brushing his teeth in the bathroom.

He stuck his head out. "You mean, she bought us presents with our money," he garbled, his mouth full of toothpaste.

I glowered at him. "Why must you be like that?"

He ducked back into the bathroom and spat out the toothpaste. "I was kidding!" he lied.

ME

Daddy says thank you.
(I further lied)

OLIVIA

I bought all the GPs cashmere sweaters I found in a thrift shop. Hope they like them!

ME

They'll love them! What grandparent can't use another sweater?

OLIVIA

I bought 1 for Preet too!

Oh my God, she was such a darling to think of him. And an idiot for not thinking how Sophie would react. I could already predict my mother's reaction to what she'd see as Olivia's throwing her money away on *that Preet,* who had plenty of sweaters from having stolen all of hers.

ME

I'm sure your gifts will bring them all much joy.

Though Neil and I had originally viewed our trip as simply to move Olivia out of her dorm and bring her and all her stuff back home, we now found we had all this extra time on our hands. We therefore decided to be tourists. Now, I might have been born and raised in the suburbs but I've been to New York City more times than I can count and have traveled out of the country as well. Still, San Francisco was a lot different than New York. In New York, first off, everyone wore black, and all the buildings and streets were gray. In San Francisco, there was color everywhere, in people's clothing, in their hair, and of course on the ubiquitous rainbow flags flying over businesses and houses, meant to signal LGBTQ-friendly premises. Even the houses were painted different colors. It was quite lovely, and reminded me a bit of the Art Deco buildings in Miami, painted in bright colors like aqua blue and flamingo pink. And as opposed to the grid of Manhattan streets, there were neighborhoods where the streets curved like serpents, or where they climbed and then plunged like roller coasters.

On our first foray, Neil and I spent the day at Fisherman's Wharf, taking in the sights and the bracing salty air. For lunch, we found a funky seafood shack where we had soggy shrimp salad sandwiches and ten-dollar beers, consumed on a less-than-pristine picnic table outside.

I must say that this was my idea, because I love sandwiches. It's my favorite food. Firstly there's the bread. I can't believe they didn't have it in Eden. All the different types are their own sort of scrumptious: soft white, whole grain, rye, cinnamon raisin, pumpernickel. Then there are all the different forms: sliced, braided, in rolls, bagels, baguettes...I am salivating just thinking about it all. Now, a sandwich takes this perfect creation and doubles it! Two slices of bread! The top and bottom of the Kaiser roll! And if that weren't enough, there's a luscious surprise in between the two portions, namely meat, tuna, maybe cheese, and often more than one surprise, for a pickle goes with the roast beef, jelly adorns the peanut butter, and mayo graces the ham or—be still my heart—sometimes aioli!

Unfortunately, our shrimp sandwiches left much to be desired. We looked longingly at bystanders scarfing down gooey slices of New York style pizza. That's what Neil had wanted to eat but I had objected to ingesting anything New York style when we were in San Francisco.

"Really!" I had scolded him. "It's like traveling to Rome and then eating at a McDonalds!"

The enticing aroma of the cheese and pepperoni assailed us with every passerby. To make matters worse, the wind kept whipping our napkins away, and my hair into my food. The sun had gone behind the clouds and we were chilled to the bone. What was it that was (falsely) attributed to Mark Twain, that the coldest winter he ever spent was a summer in San Francisco? We were both miserable as we returned to the hotel to retrieve our jackets. Once there, Neil immediately ensconced himself in the bathroom and only emerged after I had watched an entire episode of *Jeopardy!*, one hand over his stomach and the other on his head.

"I'm having my doubts about the quality of the shrimp we had."

"Really?" I responded. "I feel okay."

"You're sure it didn't taste funny to you? I feel a bit queasy."

"You mean woozy, honey. That's the beer."

"I hope that shrimp wasn't old or contaminated."

"The only thing old and contaminated is you," I joked.

"Old maybe," he parried, "contaminated, never."

"True," I admitted. "No bacteria stands a chance against your shield of supplements!"

"That's the idea," he asserted. "Go ahead and mock me, but I plan on living till one hundred."

"Well, I hope your next wife takes good care of you then," I kidded, "because I'm not planning on sticking around to wipe no 100-year-old ass. If that's my future, kill me now."

"You want me to kill you? Let's go back for some more of that yummy shrimp!" We both cracked up.

But by six o'clock, Neil's mood had nose-dived again, for Olivia still hadn't contacted us. We knew this did not bode well.

"What do you want to bet she ditches us for dinner, too?" he kvetched. We were now sitting in a French café, taking a load off our overworked feet. We had both ordered cappuccinos, and had split a chocolate croissant. It was so-so.

I sighed. "Well, let's hope not. But if she does, it's only because she still hasn't finished her project."

"Which she left for when we came here."

"She said she's been working on it for days."

"Two days," he specified. "Two whole days."

I picked up my cell phone and tried to find the right tone without appearing to nag. The white-coated waiter cleared our plates.

ME

Hi! So? What's the status?

ME

Hello?

"Don't tell me she's pulling this shit again!" Neil fumed. "Again, with the not answering?"

"Wait. She just saw it."

A few moments passed. The waiter returned to refill our water glasses.

"Oh, I see," Neil scowled, suspecting the worst. "Now she's going to ignore us."

"No, wait. Now she's typing. See? You're such a pessimist!"

OLIVIA

Hi mom. Guess what? Still haven't finished. Looks

like I'll be pulling an all nighter again. Please don't be mad!

Neil threw his arms up in the air. "Wonderful! Fantastic! We come all the way to San Francisco and the little princess can't see us!"

"Oh, Neil," I scolded him. "Try to be a little more understanding."

"No, I don't want to be understanding, Fay! Whenever she walks all over us, I'm supposed to be understanding. You just let her get away with murder."

The two women at the next table looked over at us. They were younger than us, in their thirties. Both had long, glossy blond hair. One was wearing a shift dress in dove gray, sleeveless and exposing her muscularly sleek arms, while the other wore a black pencil skirt and a white collarless top. A herringbone jacket was draped over her chair. Both sported heels—no comfy grandma shoes for them!—one a peep-toe in a two-tone gray and the other a black stiletto with the telltale red underside marking it a Christian Louboutin. I may not dress like I read fashion magazines, but I don't live in a cave, either. The sight of those two already had my hackles up and made me regret the half croissant. I didn't want to give them any more reasons to look down on me.

"Oh, so this is my fault?!" I hissed, trying to keep my voice down.

"I'm just saying she's spoiled, and that is in fact your fault, my dear." Neil never called me "my dear" unless he was criticizing me.

"I can't believe you just said that!"

"Okay, look, this is ridiculous," he exhaled loudly. "We're going to get into a fight because our beloved daughter couldn't get her shit together and finish her work before we got here."

"And that's my fault?" I wasn't letting this go.

"No," he sighed, knowing what was good for him. "It's her fault. But what the hell, we're here in San Francisco. Let's go out and enjoy ourselves."

That pacified me a bit. "Well, all right then." We asked for the check as soon as our waiter managed to tear his eyes away from the Victoria's Secret models, which took a while.

So we went to the Mission District, found a parking spot, and strolled around. For dinner, we ate one of the district's famous burritos. It was pretty good, I have to say. Neil put so much hot sauce on his (because spicy peppers kill bacteria, and are associated with longevity) that he used up my entire packet of pocket tissues. He looked like he was having an allergy attack, or like a kid who'd just heard his parents were getting a divorce.

"If that's the price of a long life," I told him, "I'll be happy to go at sixty."

"Don't forget that sixty isn't as far away as it used to be, my dear."

After dinner, we walked back to our rental car, only to find a ticket on the windshield.

"What?!" Neil was livid. "But it says you can park here!" He pointed to the sign a few feet away.

"What does the ticket say?"

"It says," he began perusing it, and then looked up at me. "It says the tires are facing the wrong way!"

"Huh?"

"That's what it says!"

Because San Francisco is so hilly, one must park one's car with the tires turned so that if the brakes fail and the car starts to roll, it will roll into the curb and not out to the street. And I thought New York was the only one that was weird about parking. They actually have signs that read "Don't Even Think About Parking Here!" Afterwards,

Olivia, who had recently gotten her driver's license, was surprised to hear that we hadn't known about tire directions. I suppose this little *fact-let* had been on our driver's exam as well, almost thirty years before, but who remembers this stuff? I've been given tickets for infractions, but never because my tires were facing the wrong way. Sometimes my tires are parked almost on the sidewalk. I am a bit spatially-challenged.

"Well, this trip is just getting better and better," Neil grumbled, shaking his head.

"And here you were saying the dinner didn't turn out to be as expensive as you'd expected," I reminded him. "Ha!"

"Yeah," he responded balefully. "Ha."

In the meantime, my phone buzzed.

GABE

Please call Mom. She's worried that she hasn't heard from you.

ME

What? We just got here last night!

GABE

I told her. But she's worried because you were supposed to call to say you'd gotten to San Francisco all right.

I sighed. She had made me promise to call as soon as we arrived, but I'd forgotten.

ME

Tell her you spoke with me and I'm fine.

GABE

Just call her. You know she won't believe me.

ME

Why the duck not?!

(autocorrect)

GABE

You know how she is.

Yes I did. Somehow I had imagined I could have a few days of peace, a respite from the Trials of Sophie, but no.

"It's so good to hear your voice! Thank God!" my mother squawked. "I was so worried!"

"Why, Mom?" I immediately launched into my counter-offensive. "You knew I was in San Francisco visiting Olivia."

"But you were supposed to call!"

"I forgot!"

"Well, when I didn't hear from you, as we had agreed," she added pointedly, "I got worried."

"You know I'm not twelve years old," I informed her, as I fastened my seat belt.

"I know that, but still, you went all the way to California, and then I didn't hear from you."

"We got in in the evening," I explained with impatience, "and we were tired, and I forgot, okay?"

"Okay, but you can't blame me for worrying!"

"But about what?" I persisted, because indeed I could blame her. "What did you think happened to me?"

"Well, you might have been in a plane crash!"

"What?" I reacted, flabbergasted.

"I know, it's silly. But you know what a worrier I am."

"But why a plane crash? Did you read about any plane crashes in California or see it on the news?"

"No."

"Exactly! So why a plane crash?"

"I don't know. It's just…when I didn't hear from you I got worried."

"But didn't Gabe tell you we texted?"

"He did, but…"

"But?" I prompted.

"But I thought he was lying!" she blurted out.

I was struck dumb for a second. "Why would he lie about something like that?"

"So as not to worry me!"

Of course. This was how my mother saw the world. Since she was convinced everything was a conspiracy, she worried constantly and read whole epics into simple, innocent responses. One could not even hide behind no response at all, for her ample and sinister imagination would heartily fill in the blanks.

"I called Mona yesterday and no one answered," she told me recently, for example. Mona was an old friend of hers.

"Uh huh."

"It's already the second time I'm calling and no one answers."

"I guess she doesn't have an answering machine. Neither do you, Mom, by the way."

"I'm worried."

"Because she didn't happen to be home on two occasions? Call the police! Call an ambulance! Call the Coast Guard!"

"Ha ha. Make fun of me, but I'm serious."

"I know you are. That's what's funny."

"Mitch has a heart condition, you know." Mitch is Mona's husband.

"Really, Mom? If Mona doesn't answer the phone it means Mitch had a heart attack?"

"Twice." *Twicccccce.* "She hasn't answered twice already. I'm so worried."

Mitch, of course, was fine. Mona had merely been out doing errands, living her life, oblivious to her obligation to wait dutifully by the phone in case her friend Sophie chose to check up on her. Still, at least it kept Sophie's mind off poor Preet for a few days.

I now assured her that we were all in one piece and that I'd see her in a few days. She asked to speak with Olivia.

"Olivia?" I dithered. "Olivia's...not with us at the moment."

"Oh, okay. Well, how is she?"

"Fine. She's fine." Neil, who could overhear our phone conversation, shot me a glance. I pretended I didn't see.

"So how does she look?"

Damn. "Uh, well, we haven't actually...seen her yet. In the flesh, so to speak."

"What do you mean you haven't seen her?" My mother's voice took on a tone meant to imply, *Don't fool around with me.* "Why not?"

"Well, she's been busy with her final exams..." I began.

"So busy she couldn't find time for her parents?" Sophie cut me off, her tone now one of disbelief. "Who flew all the way across the country to see her?" *Her* kid would never have gotten away with that shit, we both knew.

"No kidding, right?" Neil mumbled, hearing my mother's diatribe through my phone.

"Mom, it's fine. We're on our way to see her as we speak," I lied.

"Send her my love then."

"Will do. Love you. Bye!" Upon hanging up, I sighed, in relief or resignation, I don't know.

"Why do you have to lie to your mother?" Neil asked after a few moments. His question both surprised and annoyed me.

"Because it's easier than listening to her bitch at me," I retorted.

"You don't stand up to her. You don't stand up to Olivia. Always taking the easy way out."

"The *easy* way out?!" I repeated, offended. "Look, my relationship with my mother is my business, okay? Your mother is a doll compared to mine, and you know it."

"But you don't have to lie to her all the time," he argued. "It's really...sad."

"You know what?" I spat. "I lie to her because...because she deserves it, actually. She deserves to be kept in the dark, okay? Because that's what she always did to me!"

"Okay, relax." He shot a quick glance at me.

"Relax? You know, and this is just an example," I began, "one out of many, but when my dad died, she didn't let me go to the funeral. I didn't go to my own father's funeral!"

"Fay..." Neil tried to calm me.

"You know why?" I continued. "Because she didn't want to *upset* me. I spent the whole day with a babysitter!" I shrieked. "While my dad was being put in the ground, I was at home with a babysitter!"

"People don't usually bring kids to funerals."

"He was my father!"

"Look, forget what I said," Neil attempted placatingly.

But I was on a roll.

"And when my Uncle Pete died, she didn't even tell me! I was at summer camp and she waited till I came home weeks later! There I was, having the time of my life, going swimming and eating s'mores by campfire, when my poor uncle had just died! I could just vomit when I think about it! She did that my whole life, keeping things from me, making decisions for me! No, taking decisions away from me!"

"I'm sure she thought she was doing the right thing, Fay."

"I never even got to say goodbye to my dad!" My voice was breaking. Neil reached out his hand and covered mine

58   texting Olivia

with his. We drove on in silence while I stewed.

"And as for Olivia…" I trailed off.

"Yeah?" Neil prompted, eyebrows raised.

"How exactly do you think I should be *standing up to her?* You want to march over there and force her to see us? Is that what you think we should do?" I asked in a huff.

He sighed and looked over at me. We were at a traffic light. "Look, I don't know. But you know this is just typical of her, Fay. She leaves everything till the last minute, then everyone else has to deal with the consequences. Remember how she didn't pack for San Francisco till the night before? Even though we'd been hounding her to do it for days? And then she woke us up in the middle of the night asking where was her hair dryer? And how we had to buy her another inhaler on the way to the airport because she forgot hers in the house? And somehow she makes it sound like we're the ones bothering *her.* And now it's like she doesn't give a shit that we came all the way from New Jersey to help her. Like it's no big deal. Like *we're* no big deal," he concluded.

I looked at him bleakly.

He spread out his hands. "I'm just sayin'."

"Can't we just have a nice evening out," I groaned, "without for once fighting about Olivia?"

Neil turned his eyes back to the windshield. The light had turned green. "Whatever you say."

Day **Three**

ME

Morning!

(nothing)

ME

You awake?

(Evidently not. Finally, around noon):

Olivia

**Hi mom. Sorry I didn't see your message.
Like I said I pulled an all nighter last night**

ME

No prob. How'd you manage?

OLIVIA

Good! Got a lot done

ME

So all finished?

OLIVIA

Ha! I wish!!!

ME

What do you mean? I thought it was due today?

OLIVIA

It was but good news!!! The prof agreed to give me
an extension!!

ME

Till when?

OLIVIA

Tomorrow!

ME

So when do you think you'll finish?

OLIVIA

Tomorrow!!

ME

But you said it's due tomorrow.

OLIVIA

Yeah. For sure I'll be pulling another all nighter
so I'll probably finish tomorrow morning

ME

Really? So you're saying we won't see you today
either?

OLIVIA
This isn't fun for me either mom

ME
I wish you could understand how disappointing
this is for me and your dad. We came all the way
out here to see you.

OLIVIA
And I wish u could understand how stressful this
is for me. I'm already trying to get this done
before it's too late, and ur making me feel bad
isn't helping!!!!

ME
I'm not trying to make you feel bad. I'm just
disappointed that we won't see you.

Olivia
It's not like u won't c me! U just won't c me today!
Anyway we've got the whole summer to spend
together!

At that point Neil grabbed my phone and sent her a
voice message. "If we were only going to see you over the
summer, we might as well have never come!"

Voice message. Olivia, tearfully: "Daddy! Why are you
making me feel so bad?! I didn't plan for this to happen!"

"Give me back my phone," I said, grabbing it out of his
hand. "Now see what you've done. She's crying."

"What I've done? What have I done? I bought us tickets—we bought us tickets," he added, seeing my expression,
"to see our little girl and all she's done is blow us off!"

"For God's sake, Neil! She's not blowing us off. She's

trying to make a deadline. Like you've never pulled an all-nighter."

ME

Relax. Do your work. We'll see you tomorrow.

OLIVIA

Thk u so much mom!!!! Ur the best!!

ME

Love you.

OLIVIA

Love u morrrreee!!!

So we spent the day at Alcatraz, went to the Japanese Tea Garden where Neil hoped to get some landscaping inspiration, and saw the Golden Gate Bridge. Actually, we needed the open spaces of the garden and bridge after Alcatraz. They do this thing where you can go into a solitary confinement cell for a bit to see how it feels. I expected to be able to hold out for at least a little while but almost as soon as the door was heaved shut, I felt like I couldn't breathe. Not figuratively but really, I felt like I was suffocating, like I was breathing in my own exhaled carbon dioxide. I only lasted two minutes. What a nightmare.

"Remind me never to kill anyone," I joked to Neil.

We ended our evening by having dinner in a sushi bar in the Tenderloin district. It smelled of fish, surprise surprise, but the décor, a cozy mix of black and red, was tastefully done, and there were lots of customers, reassuring Neil of its quality.

"You folks visiting?"

"Yes," I answered our waiter. "We're visiting our daughter."

He mimed looking around for her.

"She must be really skinny 'cause I don't see her."

What a card.

"She's finishing up her last work for the semester," I felt the need to explain. "We're meeting her tomorrow."

"Oh. So the parents get some time alone, huh?" he winked. "Good for you."

"Yeah. Good for us." Joy of joys.

Neil was getting furiouser and furiouser.

We asked for the check.

Was I a bad mother? Was I spoiling my daughter? Perhaps it might seem I was a bit lenient with Olivia. This at least was how my mother and husband saw it. I admit that I tried not to come down very hard on her when she and I disagreed on something, or when she acted irresponsibly. I just felt that there were different ways to educate one's child, ways that didn't require beatings or screaming. Or washing one's mouth out with soap. I remember Sophie yanking me over to the bathroom, dragging me, and then smashing the bar of soap against my mouth. I of course clamped my jaws shut tight, but she still managed to pry my lips apart by pulling on my ponytail, and shoved the thing in. I gagged and wailed. She moved it back and forth a few times to mimic scrubbing, as I retched and slobbered, and then finally allowed me to spew it out into the sink, coughing and crying.

I know that in her generation, my mother was taught that sparing the rod was spoiling the child. But I ask, what's so horrible about spoiling? Isn't it preferable to traumatizing the kid? I remember my father making excuses for Sophie, that she meant well, that she was only trying to make sure I would grow up right. But even he had to admit she had a temper that she couldn't always control, and it was usually me on the receiving end, since Gabe was the baby and anyway always toed the line.

Even on my first day of kindergarten I caught a beating from her. At first the day had gone beautifully. There were toys and crayons and we sang songs and ate cookies. The teacher read us a book with pictures, and we all danced the Hokey Pokey. I loved it. It was way better than being at home under the watchful eyes of my mother, I thought. Having to share everything with my brother, having to let him have his way because he was the baby. I was glad to be away from all that.

On the bus ride back home, contented, I drifted into a daydream. I was sitting next to a window, and just gazed absent-mindedly at the houses and trees as they passed by, in my own little world. Suddenly I realized the bus had stopped but had not resumed running. I turned from the window and looked around. The bus was empty. The bus driver, way up in the front, had swiveled around and was staring at me.

"Okay, little girl," he asked. "Where do you live?"

My stomach tightened in fear and confusion. Where did I live? Where indeed did I live? I asked myself.

"Next to Denise," I finally squeaked. For it turned out that I didn't actually know my own address. The poor man had to redo his whole route, until on one corner he saw a short little crazy woman jumping up and down, frantic.

"Something tells me that's your mother," he deadpanned.

But his wit was lost on me, as I now envisioned what I was in for. Funnily enough, I hadn't been really frightened at the thought that I was perhaps lost, or that I was alone with the bus driver, a total stranger, or that I hadn't made it home. I had been weirdly calm, trusting that he would find my house. And he did. It was only when he said that about my mother, and when I saw her on the corner, her body language speaking volumes, that I began to cry. Because I knew what was waiting for me. Sure enough, not only did I get a spanking for worrying my mother half to death, as she put it, but I was made to repeat over and over our address and phone number, and then was grilled on it for days. I heard my mother on the phone the next day, relating the story to my aunt Deirdre. I heard her tell my aunt how once again I had put her through hell.

"That girl…" my mother had said, not needing to finish the thought. It was understood. I was trouble. I was a disappointment. I was hell.

When I became a mother, therefore, many years later, I vowed to myself I was never going to make my daughter feel like that. Ever. No matter what she did.

Day **Four**

ME

Will we see you today?

Frankly, my question was rhetorical because duh, of course we'd see her. She was finally finished with school! I was just phrasing it politely. I really meant, "When will we see you?"

OLIVIA

Hi mom! What a night! I'm beat!

ME

So what are you up to?
(Translation: Let's get together.)

OLIVIA

Packing!

ME

And after?

OLIVIA

I think it will take me all day!

ME

Need help?
(Again, rhetorical. That's what we were
there for, after all.)

OLIVIA

**It's a v small dorm. You'll just be in the way.
Thx anyway!!!**

"What? She doesn't even want us to help her pack? So what the hell are we here for?!" Neil, of course.

"Oh honestly," I had to lay into him. "Like you really want to help her pack."

"No, I don't really want to help her pack. But I really do want to see her before I turn eighty."

"We can drop by when it's all done," I suggested to him. "How's that?"

"I don't know. Better ask Queen Olivia."

ME

**Oh OK. So we'll meet up in the afternoon?
Evening?**
(I put in a question mark, but this was a rhetorical
question, too. Of course we'd meet up in the
evening, at least!)

OLIVIA

**Uh oh. Can't. We're all going 2 dinner w/ Rachel
and her dad.**

"What?!" Neil shouted when I read him her text. Whereupon he called Olivia on his own phone and resumed shouting. "You're what? Going out with Rachel's dad? And what about us?"

"I'm sorry, Dad! But I *have* to go. He invited us all a week ago!"

"So? We flew all the way from New Jersey!"

"I know. But it would be rude to cancel at the last minute!"

"At the last minute? You knew we were coming weeks ago!"

"I know, but it slipped my mind. When he invited us, I just said yes without thinking."

"It slipped your mind? You know how much it costs to fly to California?!"

"Dad! I was just so stressed and confused, what with finals and all!"

"Well, now you're not stressed so now you tell them you're going out with your own father and mother! And that's the end of it!"

I pried the phone out of his hands at this point. The conversation was veering off into the wrong territory.

"Olivia, sweetie," I cooed, "I understand you told Rachel's dad you'd be going but, really, I'm sure he'll be fine with you not going, especially as he knows your parents came to see you."

"Mom, you just don't get it. I don't want to be rude!"

"But you don't mind being rude to us!" Neil shouted over my ear. I took a step away.

"You know," I said softly, "your dad has a point. It's a bit insulting to us."

She began to cry. "I can't believe you guys are putting even more stress on me! Haven't I had enough with my first year in college, and with finals, and that project, and now having to pack everything up and move!"

"Fine!" Neil screamed from two steps away. "Let her go out with her new family! Just hang the fuck up!"

"Olivia," I gently probed, "are you sure you're going out

of courtesy? Maybe you would rather be with your friends than with boring old us."

"Mom! I'm going to see you guys all summer! What's one more day?"

"All right, Livy. I can't say I'm not disappointed, but whatever."

"Oh, Mom! Now I feel so bad!"

Good! But the truth is I hate to hear her cry.

"Never mind. Go and have fun. We'll see you tomorrow." And this time I didn't depend on rhetorical questions. "Right? See you tomorrow?"

"Yes! For sure! Thanks so much for understanding, Mom. I knew you'd understand."

I looked over to find Neil glaring at me.

"Try not to be so angry with her," I told him.

"With her?" he spat. "Sure, I'm angry with her, but I'm angrier with you."

"Me? How am I the guilty party?"

"We came all this way because of you, not because of Olivia!' he yelled. "It's painfully obvious that she didn't need us. *Doesn't* need us."

"Don't say that—"

"She's growing up, Fay. Can't you see that? She's going to move out of her dorm with or without us. She's going to move out of our lives," he insisted.

I was taken aback for a second. "Neil, there's a world of difference between moving out of a dorm and moving out of our lives. Don't you think you're exaggerating?"

"I'm the one who's exaggerating? The kid finds one excuse after another to not be with us—"

"They're not excuses," I cut in. "She's got finals, and final projects…"

He looked at me sadly. "I'm not just talking about now. She didn't want to go to school even in New York. They've got some of the best art schools in New York. But no, she wanted to go to California. You yourself said she couldn't find anywhere farther."

"Well, you know, California is also—"

"It's not about California, Fay. It's about Olivia wanting to leave. Like she said, she wants to spread her wings. She's our only child, and you're very attached to her. That's normal. But it's also normal that she should want to strike out on her own."

"So you're saying I smother her and that's why she wants to leave?"

He laughed. "Not at all. If anything, you give her too much freedom, and she does whatever she wants. But she's your whole world."

I stuck my chin out in defiance. "And what's wrong with that? I'm a mom, after all."

"You're also a wife, you know," he said quietly. "Maybe it would be nice for me to feel I'm your whole world once in a while."

I crossed my arms over my chest. "So what is this? You're telling me I don't pay enough attention to you? That you're jealous of my relationship with Olivia?" I hated the acidity in my voice, but I couldn't help myself. I felt under attack.

"Maybe I am," he admitted.

We remained in silence for a few moments, both of us uncomfortable with these new revelations.

"Babe, you have to let go," Neil said gently. "Olivia is leaving us. But I'm still here."

I came over to the bed and sat down next to him. I put my arm around his shoulder. "I know you are," I said. "I know you are, Neil. I'm sorry if I've made you feel...left out. But just try to be a bit patient with me. She's our only daughter. She's my Olivia. It's not easy for me."

He took me in his arms and hugged me. "I know. I know."

We stayed like that for a while. Finally, Neil broke our embrace. "Okay, look. We're here in San Francisco. This isn't just a trip to see Olivia. This is our trip in San Fran. Let's make the most of it! After all, we've got plenty of time on our hands."

I laughed, pleased to see him rebound. "Now you're talking! Anything in particular you feel like seeing?" I asked.

After thinking for a few moments, he responded, "You know what? I want to go to one of those marijuana stores."

I opened my eyes wide.

"Supposedly CBD is like a cure-all," he defended himself. "They're using it now to treat anxiety—"

"I bet!" I trumpeted. "You don't see too many hyper stoners, that's for sure!"

"—insomnia," he continued, unfazed, "even cancer. It's being used in everything now. Even dog food."

"Dog food! Can you imagine giving it to Lulu?" I suggested, referring to our aging mutt. "She'd sleep 24 hours a day, as opposed to the 23 ½ she sleeps now."

"Come on," he tugged at my sleeve. "Let's just go and see. Aren't you curious?"

So we Googled the nearest cannabis dispensary, as it was referred to. There was an armed guard in the front room, his expression as serious as a drill sergeant's, and we were required to present our ID to the receptionist, who entered our data into a computer. As I worked in a law office, I wasn't too thrilled with my name being associated with a cannabis dispensary, but it was legal, after all, so I kept quiet. Once inside, we saw a handful of attendants behind glass counters that displayed a dizzying array of marijuana-related products and paraphernalia. There were cannabis body lotions, soaps and shampoos, body washes, lip gloss and even mascara. There were vials of essential CBD oils for insomnia, for pain relief or nausea. There were even cannabis-infused drinks and chocolates. And naturally, there was a load of weed, for smoking, in a panoply of shades of green. I looked around at the other customers. We were the only ones over the age of thirty. I was tempted to buy some chocolate, but remembered a rather unpleasant experience with pot brownies once in my youth, and therefore decided to forego the experiment. Neil bought something called a tincture, that is, a concentrated extract, which I'm sure he believed would help him live till the end of time.

"It's supposed to be really good for you," he assured me. "And because it's CBD and not THC, it doesn't, you know, get you high."

"So what's the point?" I asked.

"Oh yeah, Miss Hardcore," he mocked. "Two glasses of wine and you're ready to hit the sheets. And not in a good way!"

After that we went shopping at Union Square. Neil wanted to buy a hat for the sun because he was worried about a suspicious blotch on his nose which might be melanoma. Days later it turned into a zit. In the meantime, we killed a good hour looking for the perfect SF-emblazoned baseball cap. He'd try them on, examine himself in the mirror, ask me what I thought, which was always, "It's fine. Buy it. Let's go." Then he'd look himself over again in the mirror, and decide it made his head look too small. Or too big. Or too round. Or too pointy. And if it wasn't the shape, it was the color. Red didn't go with his skin. Gray made him look sickly. Olive-drab camouflage was just horrible.

"Don't they have purple?" I innocently asked.

Neil sneered. "Only you wear purple, Fay."

Et tu, Brute?

"What does everyone have against purple?" I pondered aloud. "It used to be the color of kings."

"Now it's the color of big furry dinosaurs," he said. He finally got one in black, which looked like all the other black ones he'd been trying on for the past hour. By now, of course, it was raining.

We spent the rest of the day at the Ghirardelli chocolate factory, which had been turned into a mall, and went out to dinner at The Cheesecake Factory. I was disappointed with Neil's choice of venue—didn't we know the menu like the back of our hands? But this was to Neil a plus. At least there would be no unpleasant surprises. I was consoled by the fact that at least we'd be served some sourdough bread as usual in the Cheesecake Factory, because San Francisco is famous for its sourdough bread, and if that was the only authentic San Franciscan food I'd get in that restaurant, so be it. And then there was the view. The restaurant was situated on the top floor of an office building—Macy's was below it—and as we waited for our table, we looked out onto Union Square and greater San Francisco. Tourists were taking selfies. We did, too. Still, Neil remained angry with Olivia.

"At least you didn't have to pay for a third person," I noted, once we were seated at our table.

"Yeah," he grumbled, buttering his sourdough bread. "I hope she orders a Filet Mignon."

"You seem to have forgotten Olivia is vegan."

"No," he admitted. "I just couldn't think of an example of an exorbitantly expensive vegan dish. What would be the vegan equivalent of a surf and turf?"

"Tofu and seaweed?"

"Not expensive enough."

"In champagne reduction?"

"Better…"

"How about forbidden rice with…"

His Chicken Madeira and my Shrimp Scampi arrived.

"Um…saffron-flavored truffles?" I concluded.

He lifted his fork, onto which he had already speared a piece of his wine-smothered chicken, in approval. "Yeah, now you're talking. Hope they have that on the menu where Rachel's father is taking them."

"Hey, it's not the guy's fault," I had to say. "I bet you he dearly wishes she'd have come with us. Now he has to buy dinner for six! In San Francisco!"

This cheered Neil a bit.

Before we left the restaurant, we texted Olivia as to what time to arrive the next day.

ME

9 am? To get an early start?

OLIVIA

????? Mom, I just finished finals! I haven't slept in yeeeeaaaaars! Can't we make it laaaater?

ME

So 10 am?

OLIVIA

I was thinking more like 2

(Was that a typo?)

ME

2 pm??

OLIVIA

Actually 3 is better. I reaaaaalllly need to sleeeeeep!!!

"So I see some things haven't changed," Neil snipped. "Tell her fine. She's the one who needs our help. We'll come at three."

"At least we can sleep in," I consoled him.

When we got back to the hotel room, my mother called. "So, how is San Francisco?" she asked.

"Nice. Really nice," I answered noncommittally.

"I bet Olivia's taking you to all her favorite places. How is her new apartment?"

"Well..." I thought of lying, as usual, but Neil had shamed me, and anyway I knew the truth would come out soon enough. Still, I dreaded my mother's reaction. I imagined her condemnation once again of me as a parent, and it made me squirm. *What could I do to avoid it,* I asked myself. I decided to put a lighthearted spin on our trip, as if it were no big deal that Neil and I had gone all the way out to California not to see Olivia even once till now. Yes, I would make a joke of it. So I began with a chuckle, though my falsetto already belied my words. "You're going to find this really funny. We haven't actually seen her yet, ha ha!"

"What? You're kidding, right?"

"Nope. Not kidding," I said, sinking onto the bed. "She's been studying for finals, then finishing a project..."

"But didn't she finish school?"

"Well, yeah, now. But it's been kind of crazy...Neil's furious we've spent all that money on our trip..."

"Really? Really you haven't seen her? Are you really serious?"

"I'm serious," I assured her, a fake smile plastered on my face, as if she could see me.

"Come on!" she scoffed, her suspicious nature kicking in. "You're putting me on. Really really?"

"Really, Mom," the smile stretching tauter.

"Huh. So she just can't find the time for you, hmm? Wow. Funny."

"Right?" I readily agreed. "So funny!"

"No, I meant, it's funny how things repeat themselves. The younger generation...They just...just can't find the time for you anymore."

I sighed, partly to sound my agreement, and partly out

of relief. I had expected far more criticism from her. "Yeah, so it would seem."

"I meant, every younger generation," she added meaningfully.

"What? You mean me?" I asked, confused.

"Yes, I mean you."

"In what way am I unavailable? I am over there all the time! We talk on the phone! We visit."

"First of all, *we* don't call each other; *I* call *you*. You never call me. I'm the one who has to pick up the phone. Otherwise I'd never hear from you."

"Well, that's just splitting hairs, Mom," I answered. "You just happen to call me before I call you, that's all."

"No. Once I waited it out to see if you would call me, but by the fourth day I got worried."

"Ha. Of course you did."

"What I mean is that I had to call you because you still hadn't called. Who knows how long I would have had to wait?"

"Cue the violins," I sang, as I moved to the beige upholstered chair. It smelled like cigarettes, even though this was a non-smoking room. But if Neil hadn't noticed, I wasn't going to bring it up. Otherwise he'd start hyperventilating and make us change rooms.

"There you go, making a joke out of it," my mother complained. "Out of me. As usual."

"Okay, okay. I'm sorry," I said, not really feeling sorry at all. I was tired and just wanted to go to bed. "I get busy and I forget. I'll try and call you next time. But anyway I see you all the time."

"See? You'll *try* and call," she said, picking up only on the parts she could criticize, "like it's such an effort to call your mother."

"Are we going to get into a fight about who calls whom now?"

"It's not just about the calling."

"What else then?" I grunted, exasperated.

"Well, you said you visit me, but really, you only visit when you're with Olivia, or with the whole family. You never visit on your own."

"What?!" I sputtered in outrage. "I'm there all the time! Who took you to the eye doctor last week? Who took you to PriceSmart?"

"Those aren't visits!" she countered. "I had to call you and ask you to take me. You know I don't see well enough to drive far."

"Well, those still count," I maintained.

"No, those are errands, not visits. A visit is when you come over just to see me, just to be with me."

I didn't really have an answer for that. It was indeed true. I only "visited" if I had to.

"Well, Mom, it's not like I have loads of free time on my hands. I work, you know, and have a family. When I take you on an errand, it's like killing two birds with one stone," and as soon as the words were out of my mouth, I knew I was in trouble.

"I see," she began acidly. "So visiting me is a chore."

"That's not what I meant."

"It's almost like you avoid me."

I was about to protest that of course I didn't avoid her, when I stopped myself, because of course I did. In that moment I realized I could either continue the way I'd always done, shunning her, hiding things from her, lying to her, as Neil had accused me of, or I could be brave and be honest.

"It's just that, well," I began gingerly, "you always seem to be criticizing me. Like I'm never good enough."

"What are you talking about?" She was immediately on the defensive.

"You know, you're very critical of me, Mom," I continued. "From my hair to my clothes, to my—"

"That's not being critical! That's just a mother worrying about her daughter! That's just me wanting you to fix your hair or wear makeup so that you could be as pretty as…as I know you can be!"

"But why can't you accept me the way I want to look? Why isn't that pretty enough for you? Why do I have to be pretty the way you think I should be pretty?"

As I have mentioned, I have gray hair, which I do not color. I am not, however, unkempt. I may not wear Chanel suits (or Christian Louboutin pumps) but that doesn't mean I wander around town in dirty flip flops and ripped sweats, my hair in a scraggly bun. I go to the gym. I iron my clothes. I pluck my eyebrows and shave my legs. I wear lipstick on occasion. In my own way I put effort into my look, just not with hair dye. It's my way of making a philosophical statement about mature women, about not rendering ourselves invisible. Gray-haired men are considered distinguished, attractive even. Why can't it be the same for women? It's like middle-aged women don't even exist, like we jump from thirty to sixty and everything in between just disappears. I can spot a forty- or fifty-year-old man easily, but as for women, I often scratch my head in perplexity when I have to hazard a guess as to a woman's age. And that is of course the point, I understand. To hide one's aging, like it's a dirty secret. Frankly, I was startled and even a little stunned by other women's opposition to my burgeoning look. My mother, naturally, is no exception.

"But you still look so young!" she often protested. "You can still get away with it."

Get away with what, exactly, I wondered? With the deception, she meant. The con. In fact, I know (personally, not in some magazine photo) a mere three women who do not dye their grays. I have three lone role models. Besides those three, only Olivia and another young woman in her twenties supported my look, but then again, they couldn't know at their age the implications. For them it is still theoretical. They can't feel the fear I felt and, if I'm honest, still feel when I look in the mirror and see my visible proof of decaying. As one writer put it, the grays are a symbol of death. I aborted the growth quite a few times, actually, especially when I knew I would be meeting up with women friends. I'd panic at the last minute and rush to the salon, thinking how the other women would look down on me, as if I were "letting myself go," as if I were frowzy and slovenly. Or, worse, I imagined they'd be secretly pleased to see me so "run down," since women everywhere seem to be involved in a lifelong beauty competition, with emphasis on the word "competition." Even my mother, at seventy, will ask me, "I'm not as fat as she is, am I?" "My legs are nicer than hers, right?" We are always measuring ourselves against other women, be they in fashion magazines or seated at the table next to us.

And I haven't even begun on the subject of men. Now, Neil didn't have a problem at all with my going gray. On the contrary, he had often encouraged me to stop coloring my hair, worrying about all the cancer-causing chemicals the dyes contained. Thus, it wasn't so much that I considered how he would view me, but rather how other men, men in general, would see me, devoted wife that I am. Not that I wanted anyone else besides Neil. I just wanted to know that I was still capable of attracting someone. That I still "had it," despite the gray.

Believe me, I can hear myself. It's humiliating to think that I put such stock in what men thought of me, whether I could still interest them. I consoled myself with the knowledge that women, at least of my generation and certainly before, had been brought up to consider appealing to men as paramount, or at least high up on our list of priorities.

One of my three role models, in fact, told me that at first it was depressing, the feeling of turning invisible, no longer on men's radar. I was thus swimming against the tide of years, decades and centuries of gender conditioning, I told myself. I could afford to forgive myself the retrograde thoughts my brain splashed across my psyche.

I worried men wouldn't notice me anymore because as women we are almost invisible already. I have had men shake hands with my male companion and then ignore me. I couldn't tell if they were being rude on purpose or even worse, that they simply didn't see me as a person, as a being important enough to acknowledge. Or if they did see me, it was as an underling, lesser in terms of power, be it political, societal or merely of brute force.

Why did I say "merely?" Indeed that was the scariest one of all, as any lone woman recognizes when passing a group of men in the dark in an isolated area. Drawing men's attention was therefore a double-edged sword, for it was often unwanted attention: leers, insults, unsolicited physical contact, groping. Not to mention rape. Not to mention murder. (I read of a study once where it was found that men's greatest fear of women was that they would laugh at them. Women's greatest fear of men was that they would kill them.) Consequently I felt a certain relaxing of my defenses in my dealings with men once I had uncovered my grays. I intuited that I was no longer an object of prey. It was a liberating feeling, and not simply from a fear of violence; I felt men now dealt with me as a person, not as a sexual being, and also vice versa, it allowed me to deal with men as just people. Sex was no longer hanging in the air, be it as a fog that obscured relations and impeded friendship or a threat that made me act stilted, guarded, unnatural. Letting my hair turn gray ended up releasing me from such lifelong psychological and social entanglements.

And frankly, I was sick of hiding, of hiding everything about me, not just my hair behind the dye. I was sick of hiding my dark circles behind concealer, hiding my cellulite behind longer dresses and my flabby arms behind ever-longer sleeves. And what about my feelings? What about my opinions? I've been hiding them my whole life. In order to be polite. In order to keep my job. In order to fit in. In order to be liked. My gray locks, then, perhaps represented my own mini rebellion, my way of giving the finger to all the assumptions about me and how I ought to be.

It would seem this is how my mother saw it as well. Which for her was not a good thing.

"I just can't understand you! Look at you!" she exclaimed during one of our visits, fingering my tresses with a grimace. "Every woman in the world wants to look younger and only my daughter wants to look old!"

"I don't want to look old, Mom," I tried to explain for the hundredth time. "I want to look my age."

"But why? You could get away with looking half your age! Your face is still smooth."

"Thank you, Mom, but I really don't think I look so horrible." Yes, the hurt bleeds through my words.

"I didn't say you look horrible. You could just look so much better! So much younger."

My mother, of course, is not "letting herself go." She is holding fast onto the veneer of beauty in her standoff against the onslaught of decay. She goes to great pains to conceal her aging, and indeed, her age. Just last year, an "elderly" woman (her word) had asked her how old she was. Sophie admitted to me she had answered "around sixty."

"Around sixty?" I had asked, shocked. "You're sixty-nine!"

"Like I said, around sixty."

"Where did you go to school, Mom? Sixty-nine is not *around sixty*—it's one less than seventy! If they were neighbors, they would be sharing a bathroom!"

"Why must you be so difficult?"

"Why must you lie?"

"Because it's no one's business! And I don't look seventy. There's not a gray hair on my head, ha ha," she had retorted, referring to her dye job.

Witnessing once again my mother's attack upon my hair color choice, Olivia, bless her heart, had leapt to my defense. "You know, I heard this song the other day on my Spotify by this band called Crosby, Still…"

"Crosby, Stills, Nash and Young." *This band.* Like I'd never heard of them. Whenever I tossed out references to Billie Eilish or Dua Lipa, her eyes always shot out of her head, floored that I could be so aware of contemporary phenomena, as if I had just landed from my spaceship, or rather time machine.

"Right. Well, the song was called "Almost Cut My Hair," about a hippie who didn't want to cut his hair because he wanted to let his *freak flag fly.* I thought of you and how you let your gray hair, well, fly."

"So you're saying I look like a freak?"

"Exactly!" Sophie chirped.

"No!" my daughter jumped. "I mean yes. I mean, not *freak* like monster. *Freak* like freak accident, you know? Something unexpected."

"Well, a bit better," I conceded, "but still."

"I mean that you're unexpected, different in a good way," Olivia pursued. "You're not like those other moms with their perfectly straight, blown out hair, and their Botox and boob jobs. They all look alike."

"But they look good," I admitted ruefully.

"But you look better," she said. "I hope when I'm your age I'm just like you, Mom. Natural, honest."

All together now: *Awwwwww.* Even Sophie was touched, and dropped the subject for the rest of our visit.

Mind you, Olivia's hair is fuchsia. So much for natural. I suppose, like me, her avant-garde appearance is her way of rejecting assumptions on how she should look, of what is attractive, what is acceptable. Olivia refuses to conform to the image of the girl-next-door or the girl on the cover of *Seventeen*. It would thus seem we are alike in the way we buck the system and present a façade that is unconventional, unexpected. Yet more than just flouting expectations, Olivia's public image says "Look at me." She draws attention to herself, but on her terms. She is not a passive object. She is no longer a fairy princess. She is in control. She writes the script.

And me? Am I in control? Am I even part of the play? The other day I read an article about menopausal whales. No joke. The title was "Menopausal Orcas Transmit Their Knowledge to the Young," but it was the subtitle that really provoked my interest: "They Live More Than Thirty Years After Ceasing to Reproduce." It's newsworthy, I take it, because it is surprising that they live, and for decades yet, even after they are no longer—how shall I phrase it? *useful?*—because they can no longer procreate. The very first sentence supports my conclusion: "The reason behind the long life of female orcas, *even after* menopause, lies in the ability of the older females to transmit their ecological knowledge to the younger ones..." What is interesting to the scientists, is that the females live long lives even after menopause. Now, I don't know if this is surprising because other female animals do not live long after menopause. (Lulu's nine. That's supposedly fifty-something in dog years. She won't go through menopause, though, because she's been neutered. Does that mean she should have jumped in front of a car years ago?)

If female orcas live long lives after menopause because their existence still has value, how did we get to the point that female human beings, the supposed top of the food chain, lose their value post-menopause? I don't mean simply that they lose their value vis-à-vis sexual attractiveness; I mean they lose value on multiple fronts. They, we, become invisible, ignored. The other day someone was recounting a traffic accident and, as it occurred near my home, I asked what the offender looked like. Maybe I knew her, I thought. "Oh," the thirty-something woman answered me, frowning in effort to recollect, "I don't know. Middle-aged, I guess. I didn't really pay attention." Sigh.

It's so frustrating. If you dye your hair, you're perpetuating the illusion that middle-aged women don't exist and, as a result, erasing them. But if you don't dye your hair, you disappear into the woodwork and become invisible, similarly erased. Perhaps Olivia's got the right idea then. No one would accuse her of disappearing into the woodwork.

Day Five: **Moving Day**

After waking at five, we had breakfast in a diner. But not just any diner. It was a diner owned by one of the members of the band Green Day. How cool were we? We had grilled cheese sandwiches on sourdough. Neil just couldn't get enough of the sourdough bread in San Francisco. I was glad there was at least one thing he liked about our trip. And though it was only a homely grilled cheese sandwich, the bread was indeed spectacular, with that sourdough tang, and perfectly toasted, while the cheese melted wonderfully into an unctuous and silken dream. What more could one ask of a grilled cheese sandwich? After breakfast, we decided to go to the Museum of Ice Cream, which I had found on the internet.

"The Museum of Ice Cream?" Neil had asked in disbelief. "No way!"

"Yes, way," I assured him, and showed him the website.

"Who in hell came up with that idea?" he derided.

"Hey, if there can be a Booze Museum in Staten Island, there can be an Ice Cream Museum in San Francisco," I assured him.

"A Booze Museum in Staten Island?" he again voiced his shock. "No way!"

We found the Museum of Ice Cream, but it was closed.

Apparently their air conditioning system was down. A Museum of Ice Cream crisis, all right. I can imagine the looks on the clean-up crew.

"So maybe you can give us some free samples," Neil joked to the person guarding the entrance, "before they turn into ice cream soup!"

The attendants, however, were not amused and ushered us hurriedly back out the door.

Instead, we meandered our way around Chinatown and around one o'clock, decided to eat in a Chinese restaurant. A no brainer, you say? Not if you are acquainted with my husband.

"How about this one?" I suggested, standing in front of a Chinese restaurant which we had happened upon at random.

"We're not going to eat in the first restaurant we find, Fay!" Neil scolded me. "Let's see what our choices are."

"Fine," I accepted. "How about that one?" I pointed to the place across the street.

He gave me a look of exasperation. "Let's shop around. What's the hurry?"

Neil is very indecisive, partly because he prefers a sure thing rather than trying something new. This is why we had ended up at P.F. Chang's and the Cheesecake Factory. But Neil is also indecisive because he's a perfectionist. Faced with too many options, he freezes at the idea of choosing the wrong one, or rather of not choosing the best one. The perfect one. For he believes there is a perfect one, an ideal choice, and if he only contemplates and calculates enough, he'll find it. He believes in perfection. This is why his landscapes are always shaped and manicured in perfect squares and circles. He and Olivia have that in common, now that I think of it, in that they both have a predilection for taking the natural and deforming it, mutating it, and making it bend to their will.

"What about this one?" I offered after we had walked another block. "The Lotus Blossom Restaurant," I read out loud. It was decorated with red walls and white paper lanterns.

Neil peered in the window past the now fading newspaper reviews that had been taped to it. "There's almost no one here. That's not a good sign."

"How about this one?" The Fortune House was lit up in neon. "Plenty of people," I noted.

Neil again looked through the glass. "It doesn't look very clean."

"How can you even tell through this window?" I asked, amazed. "I can hardly see a thing."

"My point exactly," he answered.

We looked up highly-rated restaurants on our phone. But even that didn't satisfy Neil. This one was too expensive; another too cheap. Why didn't a third one have any reviews? And if a restaurant had a review, why didn't it get five stars? I pointed out places full of people. They might all be clueless tourists like us, he protested. By what seemed like the tenth block and twentieth restaurant, I finally put my foot down.

"What's wrong with this one?" I practically screeched, upon seeing Neil's scowl.

"Well…" he began. "Let me look it up."

"That's it!" I bellowed. "That. Is. It! We're going in this restaurant and that's final!"

"But…"

"No!" I cut him off. "No buts! I'm hungry, my feet are hurting me, and I just don't give a shit which place we eat in anymore!" And with that, I spun around and walked in.

Once we were seated, Neil began his diatribe.

"It's almost empty here, Fay," he said under his breath.

"I don't care."

"There was no Zagat or TripAdvisor sign on the door."

"Like I said, I don't care."

"Not even a local newspaper review."

"Whatever," I said, and put my menu up to shield me.

"It doesn't smell very clean," Neil persisted.

"It smells like any Chinese restaurant in any city in the world, Neil," I commented from behind my menu.

"Excuse me," he signaled the waiter.

"Now what?" I asked him, lowering my shield.

He ignored me, and addressed himself to our server. "I don't see the lunch specials anywhere on the menu."

"Lunch time's over," the yellow-coated waiter explained tersely. "Dinner menu now."

I glared at Neil. He had hemmed and hawed so much over selecting a restaurant, that we had missed the lower priced lunch specials.

"But it's only 2:30!" he protested.

"Dinner menu," the waiter repeated, and walked away. I didn't believe him, either, and knew we were being rooked, but I wasn't about to get up and walk out because I was famished and also because I was angrier at Neil than at the lying waiter.

"Now you know why we're almost the only people in the restaurant, genius," I said through gritted teeth. "Who eats lunch at 3:00?"

"It's 2:30!" he again squawked.

"It's actually 2:45. Just drop it," I growled, "before egg drop soup becomes egg drop of spit soup."

Neil fumed but remained silent. I ordered (what I sincerely hoped would be) egg drop soup and Cantonese fried rice. Neil ordered egg rolls and sweet and sour chicken. When it arrived, my unappetizingly viscous soup was so bland I had to add soy sauce to it. When I asked the waiter for low-sodium soy sauce, he sneered and said they didn't have any. *Weren't we in California?* I wondered. *Where every-*

one was a health nut? Then he brought over my fried rice, gleaming with oil. It had two small chunks of meat and a few paltry diced carrot pieces. I was repulsed. Neil fared no better, with two tiny egg rolls greasily slipping from his fingers and a Sweet and Sour sauce so gelatinous that his fork could almost stand up in it. We thus ate a mediocre meal at immoderate prices. They didn't even give us fortune cookies.

After Chinatown, we made our way to Olivia's dorm. Finally, we were going to see it. (Finally, we were going to see Olivia.) Her dorm was actually in Oakland across the Bay Bridge from San Francisco. We passed small but well-kept houses and I thought there was something…sunny about these houses. That was the word that came to my mind: *sunny.* I realized it was the gardens that gave that impression. Almost all the houses sported potted plants, be they humble red geraniums or the more striking violet-blue hydrangeas flanking doorsteps, while white or pink azalea bushes adorned the sides. Wisteria could sometimes be found climbing toward windows in a riot of purple. Every house, no matter how modest, was announced by a cornucopia of foliage and flora. Trees, bushes and flowerbeds filled every space. The whole image screamed of mild winters and months on end of glorious sunshine.

Besides the residential neighborhoods, there was a small main street with cozy, inviting restaurants of varying ethnic cuisines, retro clothing shops and outdoor cafes. We passed a large art supply store and a Trader Joe's. There were actual people walking the streets, unlike my own burb where the only walkers were attached to dogs on a leash, trudging to fulfill a necessity and not a desire. Here people ambled, window-shopped, and sat in the cafes littering the sidewalks. I could see why Olivia liked it here. It was so much nicer than Piscataway. It was quaint and at the same time quirky. It was so California. It was so Olivia.

We found no parking garages but managed to spy a parking spot on a side street. We were lucky to find one so close, as we knew we'd be lugging Olivia's suitcases, lamps and other paraphernalia. We chose to walk through the campus instead of on the main street because I wanted to see where she studied. I was curious to see how different it would be from Rutgers, where I had gone. Rutgers is an all-purpose university where you can study anything, from A to Z, accounting to zoology, and it sprawls over different towns and cities. It's so big that it has its own buses to transport you to and from the different campuses. Olivia's school, by contrast, was tiny, but this was only one of the two campuses, the other being in San Francisco proper, though it, too, was small. A small school, I supposed, was perfect for someone living away from home for the first time. Olivia had been right to choose this place, I thought, despite my original protests. The campus was lovely, lush and green, with winding paths. Young people meandered past us, all with their hair dyed a Froot Loops color, and most with piercings and tattoos.

"Everyone's an Olivia here!" Neil remarked jokingly, but he had a point. Olivia had found her niche, her crew. She belonged here. In this school of artists and iconoclasts, of mold-breakers and line-crossers, Olivia fit. I was starting to feel guilty about my opposition to her coming here.

We asked a lime-green-haired young man sporting a Marilyn Monroe tattoo on one arm and Che Guevara on the other for directions to Olivia's dorm. The boy kindly offered to walk us there and we chatted the short distance. He said his name was Garth.

"As in Garth Brooks?" Neil asked.

"Who?"

"Never mind," Neil muttered.

"As in Wayne and Garth," Garth explained. "From SNL."

He told us he was studying furniture making, which he enjoyed, but that he really wanted to study shoe design.

"So why don't you?" Neil asked.

"Because my parents threw a fit about me going to art school in the first place," he said. "At least with furniture, they think I'm learning some sort of carpentry, and that I'll be able to earn a living when I'm done."

Neil and I looked at each other guiltily. I thought, at least we're not the only ones.

"Yeah, parents can be…" I began, trying to formulate a blanket apology for our entire generation, only half-joking.

"At least I don't have it as bad as my boyfriend," he confided. "His parents don't even know he's gay. And he's studying business administration at San Francisco State, when what he really wants to do is learn jewelry design."

"Wow, that's different," I agreed.

"So if his parents don't know he's gay," Neil pried, "who do they think you are?"

"His best friend!" he leered, and we all laughed.

With that, he deposited us at Olivia's dorm and wished us well. We cast our eyes upon a brick building four stories high. It was nondescript except for one of the walls which had been decorated with a colorful mural of hundreds of red lips. We pressed an intercom and a voice asked us our business. We gave Olivia's name and said we were her parents.

"Is she expecting you?" the voice asked.

"You're damn right she is!" Neil squawked. Sometimes he thinks he's displaying a sense of humor by acting like a Neanderthal, and then wonders why people get offended.

I jostled him out of the way and spoke into the intercom, "Uh, yes. Yes, she is." I almost said "ma'am."

"Let me check," the intercom returned, seemingly doubting our legitimacy.

Just as I was about to rebuke Neil, a student with her

arms full of boxes approached. We watched as she tried to maneuver the boxes in order to slide her card in front of the door sensor. Seeing her predicament, I asked if she needed help.

"Um, if you could just grab my card and pass it in front of the sensor?"

"Of course," I said, taking hold of the ID card, which she wore around her neck attached to a lanyard, and passing it in front of the sensor pad. The door buzzed and Neil gallantly held it open for her, whereupon he motioned to me with his eyes to follow her. We slid past the door, and Neil offered to carry one of the boxes for her. Now I wasn't sure whether he was being gallant or conniving, as we followed the girl nonchalantly to the elevator. Well, he followed her nonchalantly. My heart beat a little bit faster, as it always did when I found myself doing something I shouldn't be doing. I am a rule follower, both because I am in the legal profession and because I am a wimp. I never cut in lines, never cheat on my taxes, never steal pens from the office. I'm not sure if it's because I'm afraid of the punishment, or afraid of the shame. So, my heart beating in staccato, it seemed like years till the elevator doors finally opened. Another person with boxes strode out, accompanied by their real parents, I assumed. I was too nervous to sneak a peak at the RA who was supposedly manning the entrance and who perhaps at that very moment was calling up to Olivia's room.

But the elevator doors closed without incident, and no SWAT team emerged when the elevator opened on Olivia's floor. Luckily I knew which, as she had complained once that the elevator had gone on the fritz and she had had to climb for two days to the top floor. We didn't know the number of her room, but each door had a sign with the occupants' names so we hunted down Olivia's. When we found it, we saw it was decorated with a collage of eyes, cut out from magazines and newspapers. I didn't know if it was meant to symbolize that the inhabitants were watching those on the outside, or if it was a commentary on the eyes of the world, or if, as there were lips painted on the side of the building, the roof would be sporting a head of hair. Whenever Olivia would explain one of her art projects to me, I'd murmur a vague understanding, because a vague understanding was as far as I ever got.

We knocked.

We waited.

We knocked again.

We waited again.

We battered the door a bit. Nothing. I looked at my watch.

"We said three, right?" I asked Neil, doubting my memory.

"She said three," he confirmed.

"Maybe she stepped out to get something at the last minute?" I considered aloud. "Maybe more boxes?"

"Call her," he said.

I did, but received no answer. So I texted.

ME

Where are you??

OLIVIA

In the UHaul, on the way to the apt!

ME

But you said to be here at 3 pm!

OLIVIA

Sorry!!! They told us we had to be out of the dorm by 2 or else we got a fine!

"Really!" Neil shouted. "She couldn't have told us before we got here?"

I duly typed:

ME
Why didn't you let us know?

OLIVIA
Sorry! Wanted to let you sleep late!

Neil barked a laugh. "*Sleep late?* Till 2:00 p.m.??"

"Simmer down," I warned him.

Me
We've been awake since 5 am!

Olivia
Whyyyyyy???
(with a crazy face emoji)

Me
(joking)
Because we're old.
(half-joking)
Give us your address.

Thus, we got back into the rental and made our way across San Francisco to Olivia's prospective abode, which turned out to be located in a very dubious area to put it mildly.... It was super sketchy.

"Sheesh! She's moving here? Is she insane?" I croaked. "That guy just pulled his pants down and took a dump on the street!"

"But just two streets away the neighborhood was really

nice!" my husband pointed out.

"Yeah, that's a city for you," I stated. "It's like New York. Just a few short subway stops separate Central Park West from the Bowery."

We stopped at a light. A homeless guy took the opportunity to wash our windshield. With his sleeve and some spit. Then he held his hand out.

"Neil…"

"What?"

"Can't you just give him some money?" Neil looked at me like I was on drugs.

"Are you on drugs?! You want me to open the window, in this neighborhood?"

"He's just a poor addict."

"An addict with a knife, maybe!" he added. "Or with a gang hiding somewhere in the shadows, just waiting for some idiot from New Jersey to open his window!"

In the meantime, the light turned green. Neil pressed the gas and the car started moving. So did the homeless guy.

"Neil…"

"Yes! I see him!"

The guy then wrapped his arms around the side-view mirror and let the car start to drag him.

"Neil!"

"What!"

"You're going to run him over! He's going to get dragged under the wheels!"

"What do you want me to do about it?!" he yelled. "He won't let go! And I am not opening this window!"

We coasted at two miles per hour, with the homeless guy literally hanging on for dear life. As if we were an inner-city float, bystanders stopped and watched our parade.

"Neil!" My voice rose an octave.

People were pointing, open-mouthed. Some were laughing. I was about to burst into tears. Neil was close to imploding. Finally the guy let go, cursing and spitting on Neil's window (but this time not wiping it off) and we barreled out of there, our hearts thudding, our nerves raw.

"I can't believe Olivia is going to live here! I don't like the idea one bit," said Neil, his voice shaking.

I couldn't have agreed more. But I tried to calm him, and myself.

"Well, she's lived here for almost a year. She must have developed some coping skills."

"She lived in a dorm. In a protected environment," he specified. "Not in the middle of a big city."

"Well, it's not like she's never been to New York," I said.

"Been there. Not lived there," he pointed out. "Big difference."

"She might as well have lived there," I retorted. "She was there every weekend."

"Well, I don't think even New York has this many homeless."

"I'm not sure you're right, honey, but maybe the part Olivia's moving to is better," I said, wishfully thinking, as we passed what amounted to a little city of tents. How did these poor people manage in the infamous San Francisco *summer?*

"Well, she's got to leave her apartment sometime, Fay. It's not a correspondence course she's taking."

Perhaps Neil was right. Perhaps it was worse than New York, or anything we were sort of used to. Or maybe it was because it was our little girl who was going to live here that we observed everything around us with fear and that all appeared to us so much more menacing than our forays into New York had ever been.

"Looks like we're not in Kansas anymore, Toto," I tried to kid, a lump in my throat betraying me.

"Lions and tigers and bums, oh my," Neil murmured.

Finally we arrived opposite Olivia's place. Unfortunately, it wasn't one of those beautiful Victorian houses we'd seen, painted in pastel colors and sporting delicate lace-like trellises like a birthday cake. Instead, it was an old, shabby structure, painted gray, or could be it was originally white and this is what had become of it. It had seen better days. As we approached, however, we saw there were no parking spaces. We went around and around and around the block, and then some, but couldn't find anywhere to park. The people in the Korean dry cleaners two spots down must have worried we were casing the joint. Eventually we were forced to pull over in a No Parking area. Neil put the hazards on.

A hotel guard, seeing our intent, approached us. (Yes, a *hotel* guard. There were hotels in this area, despite the decrepitude.)

"Sir, you can't park here."

"Look, it's just for a short time."

"Sorry, sir."

"We're just going to pick up our daughter. She's down the street."

"Sorry, sir."

"It'll take five minutes!"

"Look, the best I can do is let one of you go while the other stays, in case the car needs to be moved. Airport shuttles need this space."

"Fine. You go," he said to me. "Just hurry up."

I scooted out and up the street and rang my daughter's buzzer. I peered into the vestibule. The floors were wood, very scuffed, and there was a yellowish carpet leading upstairs. It had some sort of forest motif, but it was highly faded. Actually, the dappled leaf effect could have been an animal print blotted out by years and decades of feet tramping across it. I couldn't see well enough into the hallway, as the glass of the door was both impeded by grime and by the heavy-duty grating that provided security.

"Hello?" A voice barely audible erupted from the scratchy intercom.

"Hello! This is Olivia's mother."

"Oh hi, Olivia's mother!" the voice peeped jauntily. "I'll go get her," she said before I had a chance to ask which roommate she was.

A moment later, my daughter spoke through the intercom.

"Hi Mom! Come on up!"

"Olivia, there's no parking so Daddy had to stay in the car. You come down!"

"Oh no, Mom! I can't! I still need to put my bed together. It's from IKEA. I was hoping you guys would help."

"Well, we'd like to, but there's no parking!"

"Why don't you guys drive around the block? Maybe you'll find a spot there."

"Gee, I didn't think of that," I said in a smarmy voice. "Of course we did that! We've been driving around the block for the past twenty minutes, Olivia!"

"Okay, you don't have to yell!"

"Look, are you coming down or not?"

"I told you, I can't! Otherwise where will I sleep tonight?"

"You can sleep in our hotel room with us," I offered.

She laughed.

"Well?" I prodded.

"Oh, what? You were serious?"

"Okay, look, Olivia. Why don't we just meet up for dinner tonight instead?"

"Okay, great! Good idea! See you later then!"

"Yeah, see you later."

When I got back to the car, Neil could read my face.

"She's not coming down, is she?"

"No. She says she has to put her bed together. It's from IKEA."

"So again we came for nothing."

"We'll see her tonight. For dinner."

"Really?" he looked at me, arching his eyebrows. "Has the princess deigned to carve out some time from her busy schedule for us?"

"Just drive. Maybe the Ice Cream Museum opened."

It didn't, but by this time we were jonesing for an ice cream, despite the dropping temperatures. We therefore wandered around a bit looking for an ice cream shop and eventually found a good-enough replacement in a frozen yogurt store. I ordered a small vanilla with toasted nuts and chocolate sprinkles. Neil ordered a large coconut-flavored frozen yogurt piled high with multi-colored sprinkles, chocolate chips and gummy bears.

"I can't understand how a guy who's such a health freak orders gummy bears," I had to comment. "You do realize their expiration date is probably in the next century?"

"I know, I know," he admitted ruefully. "It's just that this whole trip is getting to me, and I just wanted something comforting, you know?"

"A teddy bear, I could see as comforting. But a gummy bear? I don't know how you can eat that stuff," I shuddered, while digging into my own healthful treat.

"It's my guilty pleasure, all right? That's why I take my supplements," he added.

"Ah, I see," I said. "Something like wearing a seatbelt while blazing down the highway at 100 miles per hour."

"Exactly," he agreed.

Poor Neil, I thought, as I saw him massage the back of his neck. The stress was really getting to him.

"Feel this," he said, stopping on the street and indicating a spot at his nape. "Does this feel like a lump to you?"

"It does feel like a lump."

He stared at me in fright. "It does?"

"Yes. It feels like one of the lumps of your spinal column. Relax. You're not dying yet."

"Ha ha," he smiled weakly, but I could see he was relieved. "Okay, now where to?"

"Oh, why don't we just walk around and kill some time till dinner," I suggested. "I saw all those designer stores on the way here, Gucci, Furla, Yves Saint Laurent....We could window shop," I added quickly, before Neil began to hyperventilate.

"Well, how about you ask your daughter what time we're meeting for dinner?" he offered. "Just in case she blindsides us again. Like maybe Rachel's *mother* has invited her out to eat." He batted his eyes in faux innocence.

"Yeah, ha ha, okay," I humored him, and texted Olivia.

ME
Hi! What time do you want to meet for dinner?

She didn't answer us right away, naturally, so we did meander our way past surprisingly full rarefied shops that had window displays sporting only two pairs of shoes or three scarves. With no price tags, of course, because if you have to ask, you can't afford it, as they say.

I admired the lone handbag in the Louis Vuitton window. It was a neat little box shape, in oxblood patent leather that gleamed.

"Ooh," I drooled.

"You like that?" Neil inquired, perplexed.

"I love the color," I explained, riveted.

"I thought you said you hated anything with the designer logo on it, that you hated paying for the privilege of doing their advertising for them."

"Yeah," I admitted. "I know. Like I said, I like the color. And the shine," I added.

"So why don't we go in?" Neil proposed.

I looked at him in confusion. "What for?"

"Well, if you like it that much," he said, "I'll buy it for you."

I almost choked. "You'll what? Neil, do you have any idea how much that bag must cost?"

"How much?"

Actually, I didn't have any idea either. "Well, I don't know. But it must be very expensive!"

"Well, let's go inside and ask."

I stared at him. "What have you done with my real husband?" I joked.

He hooked my arm into his. "Come on. Why can't I spoil my wife every now and then?"

"You know what? I don't care what you've done with my real husband," I continued. "He can go back to your planet and you can stay right here with me!"

So we walked into the Louis Vuitton store. It was filled with people. Beautiful people. People with perfect hair and perfect skin and perfect teeth, and of course perfect clothes. Swanning around, speaking in low tones, they carried Prada bags and wore Tori Burch shoes and had Burberry rain coats draped over their arms. They toted shopping bags that sported the names and trademarks of Fendi, Apple and Godiva. It was so packed we actually had to wait for someone to attend to us. In the meantime, we looked around. The store was all white, brightly and almost garishly lit. It had little cubby holes on one wall, with only one handbag in each. There was also an array of belts, and a section for scarves. While we were waiting, we gazed at the wallets and key chains before us. I picked up a small wallet. It was decorated in the trademark Louis Vuitton style, a grayish-brown with the LV logo repeated endlessly. It was half the size of a smart phone. I opened it up and out flew a little piece of paper, which fluttered to the floor. Neil bent down to pick it up. He read what was written on it, and paled.

"What?" I asked, seeing his expression.

"Oh my God, this is the price."

"It is? How much is it?"

He shook his head in disbelief. The amount was evidently so high it had taken away my husband's faculties of speech.

"Well?" I reiterated my query. He just looked down at the paper and continued to shake his head. It was as if the price had given him a momentary stroke.

"Give it to me," I finally said, and yanked it out of his frozen fingers. I looked down. $700.00. I gaped in shock. And just as I was about to say that it must be the wrong price tag, that this must be the price tag for a handbag, or possibly a fur coat, I saw the writing underneath. *Wallet*, it said succinctly and haughtily. It didn't even bother to sell itself, to demonstrate its worth, to legitimize its cost, by adding *hand-tooled leather*, or *artisan crafted*, or anything of the like. Just wallet. If you need more description, you aren't worthy. I looked up at Neil.

"Seven hundred dollars?!" I croaked. "For a wallet?" And that's when it hit me: if a tiny little ugly brown wallet could cost $700, how much could a beautiful, shiny, wine-colored purse cost? I later discovered it cost three thousand dollars. But in that moment, while holding my breath, I carefully reinserted the paper into one of the slots, tenderly folded it closed again, and gently lay the wallet down in its cushiony, dun-colored bed. I let out my breath and turned to face Neil.

"Let's go."

Outside, we raved and ranted. It was cathartic.

"Seven hundred dollars?!" Neil bleated. "Our plane tickets didn't even cost that much!"

"Seven hundred dollars!" I repeated. "You could buy a new iPhone with that!"

"A computer!" he one-upped me.

"Half a year's worth of yoga!" I chirped. Actually, it wasn't me that chirped. It was my phone. Olivia had answered.

OLIVIA

How about 10

At first I thought, "ten what?" Then I remembered we had asked her when she wanted to meet up for dinner. But can you blame me? Ten is not a dinner hour!

ME

10 pm?! Who eats dinner at 10 pm?

OLIVIA

It's just that one of my best friends here is showing his film at 8. You guys are invited too!

ME

Are you kidding me? Now you have to go to your friend's film?

OLIVIA

You guys are invited too!

"She's going to see a friend's film," I explained to Neil. "We're invited, too."

"To an art film?"

I might as well have said a snuff film, from the horror on Neil's face.

ME
(interpreting)
Daddy says he doesn't want to go.

OLIVIA
But it's short

ME
If it doesn't have superheroes or aliens, he's not interested.

OLIVIA
Ha ha! So let's meet up after for dinner.

ME
We can't wait till 10 pm for dinner! We'll be starving!

This, despite having eaten a late Chinese *dunch* or *linner* (too late to be called lunch, too early to be called dinner), and having just finished our loaded frozen yogurts-cum-crap at 5:00 p.m. But our aging bodies were used to a steady rhythm, I knew, and needed to be fed at specific hours or else all hell broke loose. I did not want to get a headache or indigestion simply because Olivia had priorities more important than us. Plus I also knew that if we waited till ten for our dinner, Neil's beefing alone would give me a headache or indigestion.

OLIVIA
But I have to go! He's one of my best friends!!!!
(Whom she had never mentioned before.)

ME
I can't believe you're ditching us again!

OLIVIA

I'm not ditching you!!! You guys are the ones who don't want to come!

ME

We came all the way from NJ to see you and haven't seen you once!

OLIVIA

It's not my fault!!! Anyway we'll see each other the whole summer!!!
(While I was pondering what to write next to get her to see some sense, she continued writing.)

OLIVIA

Btw, I wanted to talk to you about that. I was thinking I don't want to spend the whoooole summer in NJ. I'll go craaaaazy!!!

ME

You know, NJ is not one of the inner circles of hell.

OLIVIA

Are you sure??? Haha

ME

Ha ha.

OLIVIA

Really. Can't we change the ticket?

I reported to Neil her query.
"No!" he shouted. "There's no way! I bought it with

mileage. It can't be changed without paying a penalty."
I relayed the information to Olivia.

OLIVIA

Pleeeeeaaase!!!!

ME

We'll discuss this later.
(While motioning to Neil that we wouldn't.)
So I guess this is another day of not seeing you.

OLIVIA

It's not my fault!! You're making me feel so
guiltyyyyy!

ME

You should feel guiltyyyyyy!

But I didn't want to make a bad situation worse, so I
tried again to defuse the situation.

ME

So when are we going to see you? We still need to
buy you a mattress.
(I had to remind her of our worth and usefulness.)

OLIVIA

Yes!!!
(I could practically see her grasping the
opportunity to make an exit.)
Tomorrow we can get the mattress! Luv u!!!

ME

Love you, too. Enjoy the movie.

OLIVIA
Film mom. Not movie. It's not Steven Spielberg

ME
Believe me, I have no doubt about that.

As I've mentioned, at the age of around ten, Olivia was "diagnosed" by a child psychiatrist as being extremely hyperactive, which even a passing bystander could have told you. So obviously I, her mother, who had had to put up with her constant demand for action and attention for ten years, was already aware of this. I didn't need to pay three hundred dollars or answer a five-page questionnaire or flip through an entire issue of Italian *Vogue*, which is a little thicker than the Yellow Pages, while he tested and observed the girl, for him to inform me of that. What I wanted, what I needed, was to know what to do about it. I didn't worry too much about her schoolwork, because she was still in grade school and frankly, what I even remember from grade school is that I was no great shakes in the report card department, and somehow I still managed to rise up through the system and get a degree. I figured that like myself, she would eventually "get it" or at the very least get embarrassed about it, and try to improve her grades.

No, why I needed professional help was that the kid was sucking the life-blood out of me. If Olivia couldn't find a friend to play with, she was miserable, and *ipso facto,* so was I. But I didn't realize what I was in for until she started getting homework in school. To my questioning, she had a repertory of responses.

"I don't have any!"

"I forgot it in school!"

"I'll do it after I go outside!"

"I don't have to do it! I swear! The teacher said!"

"It's extra credit! That means you don't HAVE to do it!"

"I know I said that last time, but I made a mistake! This time really! You never believe me!"

And when I would actually manage to seat Olivia in front of her work, which I looked up in her Homework notebook, and which *I* took out of her book bag, from which *I* placed the open book on her desk—naturally, Neil told me this was part of the problem, that the child knew I would do everything for her, so why should she bother? But the truth is she couldn't have cared less one way or the other. If I didn't make sure it was all there and ready, she simply wouldn't do it, and I know this from experience. Thinking that my husband might have had a point, I decided not to do the usual riffling through her bag and checking up on her. For a trial period, I decided to see if, without an outside quarterback, she would go with the ball on her own. All I would do was ask her, gently, if she had any homework that day. And funnily enough, the answer was always no. In a weird clash of coincidences, for the whole trial period, she happened to have absolutely no homework. Not one math problem. Not a single reading assignment. Nada. My cynicism, as you see, was not without foundation.

Thus, every night I would verbally wrestle with my child and finally manage to seat Olivia at her desk, which we had bought for her at her request, though even I, with my love for color, could barely stomach its hideous puke-green hue. Before that, she would do her homework at the kitchen table, but there were too many distractions there; she'd get up to get a glass of water, she'd get up to grab a cookie, she'd stare out the window toward the back yard and comment on the birds. We thought getting her a desk and forcing her to work in her room would ameliorate the situation. But then, instead of having to walk over from the kitchen sink or the stove or, God forbid, the living room sofa, I'd have to climb up the stairs to her room every time she ran into a problem. At least I was developing buns—if not nerves—of steel, I consoled myself. As the years wore on, the desk was abandoned for her bed, her homework scattered all over it, competing for space with boxes of Kleenex, abandoned sweatshirts and stuffed toys, until finally she'd be on the floor, the throw rug invisible underneath her papers and notebooks, while the Jonas Brothers and the boys from One Direction looked on encouragingly from the walls and sang to her through her earbuds. By then, she didn't bother me, or just plain bother, with her studies, but when she was younger, at her desk, I would be regaled with a nightly firestorm.

"I just don't get it!"

"I can't do it!"

"I need your hellllppp!"

And if it wasn't her breaking down, it was me.

"What do you mean you can't do it? You haven't even looked at it! What do you want me to do, sit with you and talk you through it?" Which, I admit, I have done on numerous occasions.

"But I don't understand nothing!" she'd wail, dropping her head in desperation onto the desk, which she had decorated with stickers of kittens and puppies, the edges of which she'd peel off in moments of stress or ennui. Basically all the time. In fact, until the onset of adolescence and the emergence of boy bands onto her radar, her walls were always plastered with kitten and puppy posters, and her bed overflowed with stuffed versions of them. Sometimes I couldn't find her in there for all the fluffy toys. Once I almost flung our real, live dog against the wall, having mistaken her for one of her synthetic impostors. She gave me a wide berth after that for days on end.

"What do you mean you don't understand anything? So what do you do all day in class?" I huffed, standing in her doorway, my veins snaking out against my neck and my hands pressed against the doorframe, fingers white, like Samson before he brought the temple down. "Because you're obviously not listening to the teacher if you don't even know how to do the homework!"

"I do SO pay attention! It's her who doesn't explain nothing!"

"Oh, right. It's always the teacher's fault! It's never you."

"That's right!" she perked up, seeming not to have caught my sarcasm. "I hate that school! I hate all the teachers there!"

"Oh, so you think it would be different in another school, Livy?" I ventured, acid dripping from my tone.

"Yeah! I want to go to a different school!" she answered, apparently not smelling anything remotely sour.

"Well, you're not going to another school!" I sputtered in exasperation.

"Why not? You just said I should!"

"What? No I didn't!"

"Yes you did!"

We'd go a few rounds like this until eventually I'd throw up my hands, telling her if she didn't care about her education, then I wouldn't either. But as I'd be storming out of her room, nerves and vocal chords raw and shaking, wondering at what time could I legitimately open up a bottle of wine, she would now be in tears, begging me to come back, not to leave...

And so I'd forego (read: postpone) the booze, and return to her room, and we'd start all over again, but this time in C minor. Now she'd do the work, but half-heartedly and haphazardly. If I left and came back, I would find that she had skipped various questions because she just didn't know the answers, at which point I'd give in, thinking to hell with it.

Let the teacher do her job and teach her. Again. Meanwhile, her writing would be sloppy, smeared and downright illegible, but if I protested, she'd protest back, her voice higher pitched than mine, and rather than begin round three, I'd capitulate again, accepting her assurances that the teacher could read it even if I (and even she) couldn't. Whatever. The fight had gone out of me. Where was that merlot?

But it wasn't just the daily homework scuffles. There was dinner:

"Chicken? I don't want chicken. What I want is…tomato and mozzarella salad."

"Pleeeaaase!"

"Okay! You don't have to do it! I'll do it!"

"Yes I CAN use a knife!"

"But I WON'T cut myself!"

"Please please pleeeaase!"

"You never let me do nothing!!"

"Then instead I want a grilled cheese sandwich."

"But I said I don't want chicken!"

"So I'll make it!"

"But I WON'T burn myself!"

"You never let me do nothing!"

Or going outside:

"I want to play with the sprinkler."

"I don't need sunblock!"

"It's hardly sunny out!"

"But it takes so long!"

"YOU'RE the one wasting time arguing with ME!"

"Okay, okay. But I'll put it on myself."

"I do too know how!"

"I won't miss any spots."

"That was only one time!"

"You never let me do nothing!!"

Or going swimming:

"Andie and I want to go to the pool."

"Okay, we'll call her mother and ask her."

"So I'll lend her a bathing suit."

"But we don't need you there! We know how to swim! We're not babies!"

"Okay, then, you can come with us and WATCH us. Sheesh."

"What do you mean? Why can't you come?"

"What do you mean you're tired? You don't do nothing all day! How can you be tired?!"

Yes, my job was to Olivia merely a pastime, something to kill the dead hours when she wasn't filling my life with her wit and charm.

I was shocked. "But...but I'm a paralegal."

She just shrugged, unimpressed. "That's no big deal," she assured me. "Jenny says that's not a real lawyer." Jenny's mom was a lawyer. A real lawyer.

She had a point, I thought ruefully, since any lawyer worth her salt would have been able to win at least a few arguments with her daughter. Instead, life with Olivia had been one long battle of wills, and I was most often on the losing side. Usually for lack of stamina.

As for the pediatric psychiatrist, all he could do, as I sat opposite him, scanning the dizzying amount of framed diplomas perched on the walls, was tell me what I already knew (*The kid is hyperactive? Ya don't say!*) and then tell me what I didn't want to hear, namely that she should be medicated. Now, I grew up surrounded by my parents' pills slowly taking over the kitchen table as the years went by. My dad, who died of a heart attack, was the biggest drug user I knew. He took blood thinners, cholesterol blockers, anti-anxiety meds, sleeping tablets, you name it. My mother, now in her golden years, takes so many pills that she has an entire pantry shelf dedicated to them. And let's not forget Neil and his stockpile of supplements.

Neil, however, was somewhat leery of giving pills to our girl, of polluting her virginal little system with chemical compounds dreamed up by a bunch of mad scientists for the benefit of mad housewives. And of teachers, too, of course, who are the first to jump up and point the finger and push the kid to the doctor's office, in order to pursue their dream of a dazed, happy and compliant class. And talk about gilding the lily, they even become better students! Imagine, quiet, happy and studious! The Stepford classroom! (No, I'm not deriding teachers, for theirs is surely a Herculean labor—I can't imagine an entire classroom of Olivias—so I fully respect and commiserate with them.)

But Neil just could not swallow (pardon the pun) giving Olivia a pill. Supplements were one thing. They were wholesome and gentle, one step away from fruits and vegetables, to his mind. Medicines, on the other hand, were a different story altogether. They were drugs, made up of harmful chemicals, a hair length away from poison, as far as he was concerned. We debated it for days.

Neil may be a hypochondriac, but the one thing he fears more than illness is doctors. He is convinced that even if he doesn't have anything, they will find something, and if he does, their treatment will be worse than the disease. Hence he self-cures with supplements, tinctures and essential oils. Indeed, Neil was skeptical about Olivia's diagnosis itself.

"When I was a kid," he said, "there was no such thing as ADHD. I mean, there were hyperactive kids, of course, but it wasn't considered a disease! In fact, if you listen to my mother, I was probably hyperactive."

They do say it is hereditary. His mother told me my husband's childhood antics were legendary among her friends, things like climbing up on top of the refrigerator with a carton of eggs and throwing them onto the kitchen floor because he had wanted to see the chicks fly. Or betting his friends that he could jump over a cliff and land on the other side, which he couldn't and landed in the hospital instead. Things like that.

Even though I could see his point, it was often the case that if Neil said *black,* I had to choose *white.* What can I say? I am a lawyer manqué. Anyway, it keeps our relationship from getting old.

"Still," I put forward, donning the cloak of the devil's advocate, "you take an aspirin when you have a headache. What's the difference?" Actually, he doesn't, of course, but I was being rhetorical.

The difference, he explained, was that one could be purchased over the counter in any drugstore or 7-11 or just about anywhere, implying a certain benign nature that needing a psychiatrist's explicit and written prescription didn't. What if twenty years down the road, he asked, they discovered that the drug had a horrible side effect, like that morning-sickness drug Thalidomide that produced children and grandchildren with three arms and no toes and things like that? The doctor, I countered, had assured us the drug has been around for over fifty years, so something would have come up by now, wouldn't it?

"You know doctors are just the pawns of the pharmaceutical industry," Neil objected, warming to one of his favorite subjects, as we sat at the table after breakfast one Sunday. "What she needs are some essential oil of lavender drops, to calm her down."

"Oh, not this again…" I mumbled into my coffee cup, which Olivia had made for me one Mother's Day. She had painted a picture of me on it, sort of. The glazing had further distorted my image, so that it looked like a cubist portrait. The handle had broken off a while ago, so now I drank from it Japanese-style, my hands wrapped around it for warmth.

"Oh ye of little faith," Neil rebutted. "Who's the only one in this house who never gets a cold?" he asked, raising his eyebrows while leaning back and folding his arms.

"Right. Because of lavender oil," I mocked.

"Because of all the supplements I take. At my age, all my friends are on heart medications and take prostate pills. But not me," he gloated.

"Yeah I know. Super Neil, able to vacuum up an entire package of M&Ms in a single bound!"

"Go ahead and scoff, but what I prescribe is the lavender, and some beta glucan capsules, Vitamin D, and magnesium tablets."

"She barely eats her morning cornflakes. You think she's going to stuff those delicacies down?"

"You just have to be a little firm-handed with her, Fay."

And here we were. Back to my failings as a parent. I didn't need him for that. I already had my mother. I shared with her—foolish me—our worries over Olivia's doctor's prescription. She was unsurprisingly unsympathetic.

"You're letting your prejudices come before your kid's mental health," she chided over the phone. "People take antidepressants to feel better," she continued. "How is this different?"

"First of all," I countered, "*I* don't take antidepressants."

"Oh, so because *you* don't take them, everyone else should suffer?"

"How did we get on the subject of antidepressants? We're talking about something completely different!" I exploded.

"Really? How is it different?" she asked. "You are allowing your child to suffer! Because she is suffering, believe me. She gets Cs, she thinks she's stupid…"

"She does not think she's stupid."

"Oh yes, she does," my mother insisted. "She said so to me just the other day."

"What? When?" I confess that I often multitask when on the phone with my mother, as she can drone on and on, repeating the same stories, and I have a life to lead. In this case, for instance, I had been surfing the internet, skimming through photos of rescued dogs. But her comment brought me back to attention.

"When she was talking to me on the phone," my mother told me. "I asked her how she was doing in school, and she said she wasn't doing well because she's not as smart as the other kids."

"Oh my God, Mom. Is that what she said?" I was heartbroken.

"That's what she said."

"Why didn't you tell me?" I demanded. "You should have told me, Mom!"

"I didn't want to upset you."

"You didn't want to upset me? She's my daughter, for God's sake!"

"Well, now you know what to do about it. So she won't have to feel like she's stupid, like she's a bad kid…"

"I never make her feel like she's a bad kid!"

But I stopped myself. *I* might not make her feel like a bad kid, but I knew plenty of teachers who did. Olivia's English teacher, Mrs. Swoboda, had used up entire forests writing notes to me about her behavior, using words like "disruptive" and "bothering," which, let's face it, don't tell a parent a damn thing. How are you to correct a kid (read: punish), which is supposedly the reason for the note, if you only have a vague complaint from the teacher, as opposed to your own child's version of events, which is invariably wildly different? Well, you can't say the teacher is lying, which is tantamount to shooting yourself in the foot, but you're not about to call your kid a liar, either. After all, you weren't there, so how can you contradict her version without essentially implying that you don't ever believe a word she says? You don't need to read a book to know how much that would screw up a kid's self-esteem. Basically, since you weren't there, your hands are tied. So why waste paper?

I had even gone in to talk with Miss Norland, the homeroom teacher, and explained my confusion over the fact that she never sent me notes about my daughter's behavior, as opposed to the English teacher, who did, and how. I asked her, did she think Olivia misbehaved in English class because she was already naturally talented in English (as you can plainly see, the girl has a gift for gab), so she felt she could goof off and get cocky? Or was she perhaps bored in the class for that reason, and thus acted out?

She explained to me that in fact, Olivia was no saint in her classes, either. She told me Olivia would stand up in the middle of class, while Miss Norland was talking, calmly cross the room in front of her, and fish through her cubby. When Miss Norland scolded her, she looked at her innocently and said, "But I needed a pencil."

"So you raise your hand," she had suggested.

"But why? You're only going to tell me to get one from my cubby."

"But you need permission," the teacher had insisted.

"I didn't want to interrupt you. That would be rude," Olivia had answered.

I hadn't heard about this episode because, Miss Norland explained, she and Mrs. Swoboda evidently had different philosophies regarding discipline. The English teacher, she assumed, felt it was the parent's job to impose discipline on the child, and thus whenever Olivia behaved inappropriately, Mrs. Swoboda felt it was her duty to inform the parents and let them decide which action should be taken. (Which, as I explained above, is useless. So teachers, if you're out there, don't try this at home.) Miss Norland, on the other hand, was of the opinion that what happens in Vegas, stays in Vegas. If the infraction occurs in school, the punishment should be meted out then and there as well. Thus, she told me, when Olivia did something wrong, she would keep her out of recreation period for five minutes. After a while, the mere threat of punishment was enough to keep her in line, like an anti-bark collar for a dog. Now, five minutes may not sound like a lot to you, but for any child, much more so a hyperactive one, to miss out on her favorite time of the day, namely recess, and to have to remain attached to a chair for five whole minutes (that's three hundred seconds!), immobile, while she can hear her cohorts outside, free and unfettered, whooping and kicking and whatnot, well, that's just inhuman. It's enough to break any kid. The woman was a genius.

"I feel," Miss Norland had said, "that it's the teacher's job to deal with the discipline in school, not the parent's."

"And that's why we love you," I had responded in complete earnestness. I think I may have even kissed her.

But there I was, facing a different authority on children. My mother.

"You're being totally selfish," she upbraided me.

"We are only looking out for Olivia's best interests," I said defensively, squirming in my chair. We had been on the phone a while and my butt was becoming numb. It was supposedly an ergonomic chair, but I had gotten it at Walmart. Penny wise and dollar foolish indeed, the screws magically seemed to unscrew themselves and pop out at irregular intervals, leaving the back lopsided and the seat to suddenly fall or rise at its whim.

"No, you're not," she shot back. "You're not giving her the medicine that would let her fulfill her potential!"

"You know, Mom, the pill doesn't actually make a kid smart."

"I didn't say it makes a kid smart. Olivia is already *smartttt*," my mother spat. "The pill will allow her intelligence to come through."

"I just…" I floundered for words. "I just can't see giving her a pill as if she has a disease," I finally clarified.

"But it *is* a disease, don't lie to yourself!" she shouted. "Some part of her brain is not working right, and the medicine will fix it and allow her to calm down and be a success. What is so wrong with that?"

"Well," I began wrapping up, "I'll think about it." This was one of my stock phrases, a veritable get-out-of-jail card. Whenever I wanted to shut someone up, whenever I wanted to terminate a conversation, whenever I wanted to end a disagreement without giving in to the other side's argument or without being obliged to promise anything, I told them, "I'll think about it." It was the ace up my sleeve, and the only one who had ever seen through my stratagem was Olivia. I can't remember how old she was when I used it yet again and she yelled, "No! Don't think about it! That always means no!" As with the emperor's new clothes, only the child could see through the flimsy subterfuge.

In the end, I was swayed not by my husband, nor by my mother (though despite not being an MD, at least she was a mother. I took Olivia once for an entire month to a highly recommended child therapist, a *psychopedagogue,* if you can wrap your tongue around that, until I found out she didn't even have children! That's like being a photographer and not owning a camera!). I decided finally to listen to the doctor, and to at least try the medicine. After much debate and discussion, Neil and I agreed to give Olivia the pills for a month, as a trial.

We waited with bated breath, day after day, eyeing our

test subject with close scrutiny, while nonetheless trying to appear nonchalant, so as not to produce a placebo effect. We told her it was a vitamin.

"Like Daddy's?" she had asked.

"Yeah," I responded. "Except you only have to take one, not fifty."

If there was an improvement, it was subtle at home, though Olivia did seem a bit calmer. In school as well, the effect wasn't night and day, apparently, but rather mild. The teachers didn't know about the treatment, again so as to avoid placebo interference, but nonetheless lauded Olivia's newfound calm and obedience. Then again, her teachers would always fall all over themselves to tell me about Olivia's improvement when Neil would put the fear of God into her and tell her to mend her ways or suffer the consequences. Neil's threats and punishments would have a similar effect, in that she would calm down for a few days or a week, much to the delight of her instructors. But then eventually Olivia's wild side would rear its ugly head and the idyll was over. Ergo I was cautiously optimistic about the teachers' comments, and we might have gone the distance on the treatment, I think, were it not for one thing: the meltdowns.

They began about a week or a week and a half into the treatment.

"Mommmmm! I can't find my red paaaaants!!!"

"That's because they're in the washing machine."

"But I want to WEAR them!"

"So wear something else."

"But I WANT to wear the RED ones!"

"Then wait till they're done."

"That will take FOREVER!"

"No. It will take thirty to forty minutes."

"Waaaaahh!"

"Olivia! Don't you think you're overreacting?"

"WAAAAHHHH!"

"Olivia! Really!"

"WAAAAHHHHH!!!!"

I was used to Olivia's ravings, but this was a new level of hysteria. Usually she argued and argued with me until I gave in or compromised or at least distracted her. But she never started wailing like this. It didn't take long before I put two and two together and realized that it was the medicine. The drug would wear off sometime in the evening, and suddenly every evening, around 6:00 p.m., Olivia would have a sobbing fit. Over anything. Once because her friend went into her room without permission.

"But I didn't let Janice go in!"

"Okay, I understand, but it's not such a big deal, Liv."

"But she just went IN!"

"I get that but—"

"I didn't LET her! She just went IN! WAAAHHHH!"

Poor Janice's mother had to come pick her up before the arranged time.

Another time because her father and I were going out to dinner:

"But I don't want you to go!"

"Olivia, we'll be back before you know it."

"Don't GO!"

"Olivia, you and your babysitter, Cindy, can do fun things while we're gone."

"Pleeeeeeaaaase!"

"Remember how last time you made those origami butterflies?"

"Don't LEAVE me!"

"Cindy says she's going to teach you how to make flowers with colored tissue paper!"

"WAAAAAAH!"

It didn't take much. It's like she was hunky-dory while

on the drug, but as soon as it wore off, she became overly emotional, ten-fold, like a menopausal woman watching *Steel Magnolias*. It was heart-wrenching. To see your kid breaking down like that, sobbing inconsolably, for a half hour at a stretch, completely and utterly bereft, as if her dog had died, it was too much. Up until almost the end (for we suspended the treatment on day twenty-seven), she was just beside herself with anguish—at six o'clock—every night. Every single night. Olivia may have been suffering to a certain extent before the pills, but that was nothing like the suffering she was experiencing every night *on* them. Not to mention us.

My mother, of course, would remind me that she raised two children practically alone, and lived to tell the tale. What a whiner I was! With only one kid!

"I spoke to Betty the other day," she said, again during one of our phone conversations, Betty being an old friend of hers. "She said she had eight grandchildren, four from Eugene and four from Mandy."

"Four! They had four kids! Jeez, I'm half-suicidal from only one!"

"Don't say such things, even as a joke," my mother berated me. "Anyway, you don't hear them complaining."

"You mean *you* don't hear them complaining. I bet they do a lot of complaining. Loads. Truckfulls."

"Really," she breathed, in exasperation. "You should consider yourself lucky to have such a wonderful daughter."

"I do! I do!" I protested guiltily. Rather than pursue this down the rabbit hole, I thought, better to change the subject: "And what about Leah," I asked, since she hadn't mentioned Betty's middle daughter.

"Oh, she said they didn't *want* kids." She paused for effect.

"And?" My mother's silences are always pregnant (forgive again the pun) with meaning.

"And…" she responded, "who doesn't want kids?"

A sane person?

"Mom, there are plenty of people who don't want kids."

"Oh please." And with those two words she dismissed an entire subsection of the world's population. "Maybe it's that they can't have kids. Or maybe Leah's divorced and Betty didn't want to tell me."

Notwithstanding my mother's implications that I should quit my moaning when it came to raising Olivia, whenever she babysat for us it was a different story. She'd meet Neil and me at the door at the end of the evening with a wild-eyed look, her voice ragged, asserting, "I just don't have the strength!" After a few years, we had to stop using her as a babysitter.

Well, we also stopped asking Sophie to watch Olivia for a different reason. One night, we came home and as usual asked her if all had gone okay.

"Oh yeah, it's okay now," she stressed. "Olivia's in bed, asleep."

"Terrific, Mom," I said. "Thanks."

"But let me tell you," she continued, stuffing an arm into her black faux fur coat as she prepared to leave, "she sure raised hell about going to bed at nine. She kept refusing and wouldn't listen to me."

"I see."

This was par for the course with Olivia. My mother had her coat on now. It practically scraped the floor, as she was so short. Neil opened the door to usher her through. It was his turn to drive her home.

"So I had to give her a little smack," she concluded.

Neil and I both froze. "You what?" I gasped.

"I smacked Olivia on the bottom for misbehaving," my mother calmly declared.

I was appalled. Neil stepped outside, giving me a meaningful look. She was my mother. I was left to deal with this.

"Mom," I began as steadily as I could, "we don't believe in corporal punishment. You know that."

"Oh, a little smack never hurt anyone." She flipped her hand in the air in dismissal. "I didn't hit her in the head or anything. Just on her butt."

"Mom! I don't care where! I do not allow anyone to hit my child!"

I felt and saw my face redden as I glanced at the entryway mirror, a huge panel taking up almost the entire wall, which had to be replaced twice due to Olivia accidentally slamming into it. But Neil kept replacing it, an optimist to the end.

"I'm not anyone," my mother huffed, folding her arms, offended. "I'm her grandmother."

"I don't care if you're Michael Jackson!" I snarled, immediately regretting the comparison. "We don't allow anyone to hit Olivia."

"Well, no wonder she's so badly behaved."

"She's not badly behaved," I snapped. "She's got ADHD."

"Yeah, yeah, now you want to blame the diagnosis," she mocked. "But all she had to do was cry a little and you took away the pills."

"Cry a little? Mom, you didn't see—"

"It's because you don't show her who's boss that she gets away with murder."

"She does not get away with murder, and we don't allow anyone to hit her."

"Well, I hit you and you turned out all right, don't you think?"

I didn't answer.

Day **Six**

The next day when we called, Olivia's phone didn't answer, and the texts we sent were unseen. Jeez, till what time could that girl sleep? It wasn't until noon that we finally heard from her.

OLIVIA
Sorry! I forgot to charge my phone last night!

"She forgot to charge her phone?!" Neil bleated in the background. "Bullshit!"

"Shhh!" I berated him. "It could happen."

"No it couldn't!" he retorted. "She's attached to that phone like it's an IV!"

"Just forget it," I said to him.

ME
When should we pick you up to go get the mattress?

OLIVIA
No need! Rachel's father took us to IKEA and I

bought a mattress that rolled up into a small package. I'm all set!

Rachel's dad was starting to get on my nerves.

"Does this smell clean or dirty to you?" Neil asked as he thrust a pair of his underwear at my face. The red and blue Tommy Hilfiger label loomed toward me.

"Get that thing away from me!" I barked, slamming his arm away. I almost backed into the mirror-encased closet door.

He laughed. "I just want to know if it's one I've already worn or not."

"Really?" I chided. "You just throw dirty and clean underwear together?"

"No, but I think I might have tossed it in with the dirty side of my suitcase by mistake," he explained. The bed sagged as he sat down on it.

"And you wanted me to be the one to smell it?" I asked incredulously.

"You know I don't have a good sense of smell."

"Well, too bad!" I brayed. "I love you, but not that much! Now stop bothering me," I ordered. "I'm texting Olivia."

"*Texting Olivia,*" he repeated dreamily. "Maybe they'll put that on our tombstones."

ME
(Typing while eyeing Neil with dry amusement.)
So what about lunch?

OLIVIA
We already ate. But you guys go have lunch and I can take you sightseeing later!

ME
You sure you have time for us?

(I texted bitchily)

OLIVIA
Don't be like that mom

Since she wrote without punctuation, I at first thought, which mom?

OLIVIA
I can take you to alcatraz!

ME
We went there already.

OLIVIA
Oh. Then I'll take you to the mission district

ME
Ate a very expensive burrito there.

OLIVIA
Boy you guys sure got around! So we can go to the tenderloin

ME
Been there.

OLIVIA
Wow! The golden gate bridge?

ME
Yup.

OLIVIA

Fisherman's wharf?

ME

Daddy has sunburn as a souvenir.

OLIVIA

Ha ha! Well, we could go to union square. It's a
nice shopping area.

ME

Saw it. We've been to the Japanese Tea Garden, to
Ghirardelli's, saw the Painted Ladies...

OLIVIA

Ok. So maybe just dinner?

ME

Sounds like a plan. Pick you up at 7?

OLIVIA

Great! Can't wait 2 c u guys!!!

Then a few hours later:

OLIVIA

Mom. Can we make dinner later than 7? Some
friends from fashion design are having a fashion
show and one of the models can't make it so they
asked me to fill in!!!! I'm going to model!!!!

"Not again," sighed Neil, beaten down.

ME

What time?

OLIVIA

They said it would end after 9

ME

Fine. Text us when you're finished.

But at 9:00 p.m., we hadn't heard from her.

ME

Olivia?

Nor at 9:30 p.m.

ME

Hello?

Sure enough, it was 10:30 p.m. before she contacted us.

OLIVIA

Hi mom! Sorry it's so late! We just finished!!

ME

How was it?

OLIVIA

It was so great!!! I felt like a starrrr!! They did my
makeup, and my hair! I wore a yellow dress that
set off my blue hair! Wait till you see me!!!

ME

Wait, what? Your hair is blue now? I thought it

was pink!

OLIVIA

Now it's blue!
(I just shook my head, though she couldn't see me.)

OLIVIA

So when do we meet?

ME

Livy, we ate already! It's almost 11! We're
already in bed!

OLIVIA

Oh! Too bad!! But I understand

ME

Thanks.
(She didn't catch the sarcasm.)

OLIVIA

But don't worry. I posted the photos on my
Instagram so u can c them!!!

ME

That's a relief.

OLIVIA

Are you being sarcastic?

ME

No. I'm just tired.

OLIVIA

Oh. Well get some rest. C u tomorrow!!! Can't
wait!!!

ME

Of course you'll see us tomorrow! You're traveling
back home with us! Or are you going to miss that
too?

OLIVIA

Ha ha v funny!

Our flight was at 7:00 p.m., which meant we had to be
at the airport at the latest by 5:30 p.m., which meant Neil
insisted we be there at 4:30 p.m., since we had to return the
rental car and anyway you never knew. But I was sure he'd
make us get there by 4:00 p.m. because of his nerves. Fine.
Whatever. We were to pick up Olivia from her apartment
at noon.

ME

12 pm? Why so late? Why don't we have breakfast
together?

OLIVIA

It's my last night!! I wanna have fun!!

ME
(groaning)

Fine. See you at 12.

OLIVIA

Btw mom have you thought about what I said
about changing the ticket?

ME

Daddy says you can't. He bought it with mileage
so there's a penalty.

OLIVIA

Well I called the airline and they said there's no
penalty and that I can change it

ME

What? Are you sure?

OLIVIA

Yep

ME

But why do you want to change your ticket?
Don't you want to see your old friends?

I knew by now that we weren't going to swing the vote
by ourselves.

OLIVIA

Mom my life is here now

ME

So when do you want to go back to SF?

OLIVIA

After 2 weeks?

ME
(despondent)

2 weeks?? But what are you going to do all
summer there?

OLIVIA

Gee I bet there's nothing to do in SF

"Why does she love this place so much?" Neil bellyached. "It's full of homeless. Some of them might be dangerous!" I related to her her father's comment.

OLIVIA

Every place has homeless! NY has homeless! Even NJ has homeless!

ME

There seem to be more here.

OLIVIA

Mostly they're harmless mom. But some people just freak out when they see them. Our friend Beth came over last night and told us the most hilarious story of some homeless guy hanging on to some old couple's car and them dragging him half a block! Instead of just opening the window and giving him some change! Tourists!

We both colored as we stared at each other in complicit silence, which Neil finally broke.

"So she just wants to laze around all summer in San Francisco and we have to pay for it?" he sputtered. "Is that it?"

ME

Daddy says it's expensive for you to spend the summer in SF.

(I translated)

OLIVIA

I'm gonna get a job! Stephanie said there's an opening in the coffee shop she works in!

I paused, defeated. Why was she so set on not spending the summer at home?

OLIVIA

You guys always say you want me to be more responsible!!

"Yeah, well, if she's gonna spend the summer in San Francisco," Neil growled, "she better get a job 'cause I'm not paying for it."

ME

If you get a job then OK.

OLIVIA

Yay!!! Love uuuu!!!

ME

Love you, too.

(Despite it all.)

See you tomorrow.

As I already expected, my mother called after dinner.

"So," she launched in immediately, "have you seen Olivia?"

I was at this point too embarrassed to tell her the truth, but also too embarrassed to lie in front of Neil, so I finessed it.

"Her hair is blue now."

"You're kidding."

"Nope. Peacock blue. I was shocked, too."

"That girl…is just out of control."

"Oh my God, Mom. It's just hair dye."

"Gosh, between the two of you…"

"What do you mean, the two of us? Now what have I done?"

"I just meant about your gray hair."

"Oh, not that again."

"If you only took a little more care of your appearance…"

"I do take care of my appearance!" I answered, raising my voice. Neil, sensing an emotional outburst, hoofed it to the bathroom and sequestered himself there with his cell phone. "Why can't you respect my choices, Mom?"

"Oh, why can't I respect your choices? Oh really? Weren't you just the other day moaning about Olivia and her tattoos and piercings and weird hair color? Hmm?"

"Well," I sputtered, "there's quite a difference between tattoos and piercings and blue hair and just not wearing makeup or letting your hair go gray."

"Really? I don't see the difference. I complain about your gray hair and you complain about Olivia's pink or blue hair. We both want our daughters to look a certain way. Why is it okay for you to complain but not me?"

"It's not the same!" I countered.

"It is the same! You're shocked by Olivia's blue hair like I'm shocked by your gray. I'm not used to women not dying their hair. Just like you're not used to them dying them blue. It's exactly the same. We both want our daughters to look… you know, good. Appropriate."

Oh my God, I suddenly realized, she was right. I was repeating my mother's behavior, just in a different octave. My mother dyes her hair to look younger; I refuse to dye my hair in order to look like myself; and Olivia dyes her hair in colors heretofore unknown in nature to look however the hell she wants to look. Have I learned nothing from my own battles with my progenitor when I try to convince my daughter not to dye her hair because she looks so beautiful naturally? To me. She looks beautiful naturally to me, but that's not the point, is it? Olivia's right, it shouldn't be about what I want. And it took my mother haranguing me to see this.

But of course I couldn't admit this to her, so I pressed on. "You know, Mom, it's not the same thing because it's not just how I look that you disapprove of. I feel like my whole life, you've criticized everything about me. From my friends to my boyfriends to my career…"

"Oh, come on. I didn't criticize all your boyfriends or friends. Only the ones who were no good for you. That's my job! To look out for you. Michelle, I love. But remember that Joanne? She was a very bad influence. And look how she turned out. I was right about her." Joanne had gotten pregnant before even finishing high school. She had the baby, her boyfriend left her, and the last I knew she was still living with her parents and working three jobs to support the kid.

"And as for boyfriends, the one I liked the best is also the one you liked the best because you married him! So I guess I must have been right about him, too." I could practically see her smirk through the phone.

"Fine. And what about my career?" I continued. "I wanted to go to law school, but no. You wouldn't let me."

"I wouldn't let you? If you really wanted to go to law school, you could have gone."

"What?" I practically shrieked. "You said law school was too expensive! You said it would take me too long!"

"Well, it was expensive, and it would have taken you longer than becoming a paralegal. You know we didn't have much money since your father died."

"But Gabe became a lawyer."

"Well, he's a man."

"So?"

"You know, honestly, you didn't really hear about women becoming lawyers then. A woman had to raise the family. She couldn't afford to spend years studying and then working long hours."

"Oh, Mom," I sighed. "It shouldn't have made a difference. I'm a human being, too. I should have been able to choose what I was going to do for the rest of my life."

"Okay, see? There you go again. You only see what I do as bad, but when you do the same thing, it's okay."

"What are you talking about?"

"'Olivia wants to study art, oh no! How is she going to earn a living?'"

"I didn't say that."

"You did so! You told me you were so worried that an artist wouldn't be able to support herself."

"Weeeelllll…" I stuttered, "there's a world of difference between your kid wanting to be a lawyer and wanting to be an artist. You never hear the expression *starving lawyer.*"

"Tomayto, tomahto," she replied.

"Oh, just forget it," I spat.

"Oh, you're such a hypocrite."

"Mom, it's getting late. Why don't we continue this another time, okay?"

"Fine," she sighed. "Kiss Olivia for me."

"Will do." If I ever see her.

Neil, who had emerged from the bathroom upon noting a de-escalation after I hung up, now shook his head.

"What?" I demanded.

"You and your mom," he answered, still shaking his head.

"What about me and my mom?"

"You're always so down on her," he replied. "I really don't see why."

"I guess that's because you didn't grow up with her."

"Why? What did she do to you? Did she torture you? Did she abandon you?" he asked sarcastically.

"No, she didn't torture me," I answered, annoyed. "But you really don't have a clue what living with her was like."

"Seems I've heard enough over the years."

I groaned. "Well, what can I say? My mother is very complicated."

"Really? I don't see that," he blithely replied.

Of course he didn't. Sophie was always sweet as honey with Neil. Because he was a man. Or because he was anyone but me. Everyone loves my mother. All they see is her million-dollar smile, all they hear are her cute little jokes. She is always on her best behavior with the rest of the world. Neil, at least, saw how she was with me, but always felt I was too sensitive to my mother's barbs, that I exaggerated her reproaches, and that I just needed to ignore her knocks and swipes and grow a thick skin. But I can't.

"Again, you didn't grow up with her," I said as we walked to the car. We had decided to go to the movies, to see the latest *Avengers* film. Neil's selection, obviously. "You didn't grow up hearing her condemn you for every little thing."

"That's not what I see."

"Oh? And what do you see?" I asked. We were now in the car, and I leaned back toward the window and twisted myself to face him.

"I see a woman who, like yourself, was only able to have one daughter, and therefore showers attention—both good and bad, granted—on that beloved daughter," he responded, as he turned to me and smiled.

"It's not the same. She is very critical. I don't think I am."

"No, that's for sure, you're not critical *enough*," he declared, "but that's another subject. I'm just saying that if Sophie criticizes you, I think it's because she worries about you."

"But why? Why should she worry about me?"

"Ha! Why should she worry? Your mother worries about everything!"

I grimaced in an attempt to smile. "Now that is true. But whatever the intention, living under an umbrella of disapproval is no picnic, let me tell you."

"No, but if you know why she does it, you should maybe be a little more understanding of her. A little more forgiving."

"I am not…I mean, I don't need to forgive her for anything," I reacted, flustered.

"It seems you do. It seems to me that you are a wee bit angry with her, frankly. You hardly have anything nice to say about her."

"I…Really? Is that how you see it?"

"Um, yes," he replied, distracted.

"Well, I'm sorry you think that but honestly, that is not true."

"What isn't true?" By now he had practically forgotten what we were even talking about, engrossed in finding a parking space.

"That I…I don't know. That I don't have anything nice to say about her."

He just looked at me, raising one eyebrow as a rebuttal.

We parked and walked to the cinema in silence, and then stood in line for popcorn. I waited till we were more or less out of earshot.

"Well, now I feel really bad," I began, lowering my voice, "that you think I don't love my own mother."

Neil didn't answer as we searched for our seats.

"Did you hear what I said?" I prompted him.

"What were we talking about?" he murmured.

"That I don't love my mother! According to you."

"Oh, I don't think you don't love her," he replied with equanimity. "I just think you're a bit...uncommunicative with her. And maybe a bit angry with her, too." The lights went down, and the previews began.

"Well, maybe I am a bit uncommunicative," I conceded, recalling my mother's recent accusations. "But as for angry...I don't know. Am I angry with her?" I asked, lowering my voice again.

"Shhh," he scolded me. "I love the previews."

I remained quiet. For a few moments.

"I do not think I'm angry with her," I whispered.

"Whatever," Neil cut me off. "Just let me see the previews."

"Really?" I retorted. "The previews are more important than my relationship with my mother?"

Neil sighed. "At the moment? Yes."

"So you think I'm angry with her?" I wasn't going to let this go.

"Frankly, I think you are," he insisted. "Happy? Now can we just watch the previews?"

"Happy? How can I be happy?" I asked. "Why? Why do you think I'm angry?"

"Maybe you should ask yourself why," he whispered. "Now be quiet. It's starting."

I was quiet...for a minute. But then:

"I do know why I'm angry with her! It's like you're taking her side."

"Come on, Fay! I'm not on anyone's side! Can't we discuss this later?" he suggested through clenched teeth.

"How can I concentrate on a stupid movie now?" I retorted. "When you think I'm such a bad daughter?"

"I didn't say you're a bad daughter," he whispered hoarsely. "I'm just saying she's only human, you know. I'm sure she's done the best she could. Now let's drop it!"

"Shhhh!" Someone behind us hissed.

Neil gave me a dirty look. I reverted to silence, cowed. But I couldn't hold it in for long.

"Wow," I whispered. "This is certainly weird, you lecturing me on my relationship with my mother."

This time he didn't answer. The movie ran for a while but I stewed, unable to concentrate on the film. Except for the scenes with Thor, which somehow managed to distract me a bit.

"So you think my problems with my mother are all my fault?" I resumed after a while, in a low undertone.

He blew out his breath in exasperation. "I didn't say that. Can we please continue this later?"

"Shhhhh!" Again from behind us.

"You know what? Fine. I'll meet you outside after the movie's over," I spluttered, angrily rising.

"Hey!" the jerk behind me protested. "Sit down!"

"Oh, just shut up!" I blurted, close to tears.

"No, you shut up!" he yelled. "We're trying to watch a movie here!"

"Fay!" Neil grabbed my hand, but I wrenched it away.

"Enjoy your movie!" I spat.

"I wish we could!" interjected the jerk behind us.

"I wasn't talking to you!" I threw out as I exited the row.

"I wish you weren't talking to anyone!" he shot back.

By now I was on the verge of tears, and I didn't even know why. Because Neil had implied I was a bad daughter? Because he didn't understand how my mother got to me? I tried to get myself under control as I stood outside the bathroom. Neil was soon beside me.

"Honestly, Fay! What's the matter with you? Can't we just watch a movie in peace?"

"Hey, don't let me stop you! Go in and watch your movie!" I started to march away.

He grabbed my arm. "Fay," he began, moderating his

voice. "Honey. What's the matter?"

"What's the matter?" I began. "What's the matter? What's the matter is that you think I'm a bad daughter!"

"I never said—"

"And you know what?" I continued. "You're right! I am a bad daughter!"

"Fay, no you're not—"

"I am! I don't appreciate my mother. I push her away."

"Look," Neil tried again, "can't we go over this later? We're missing the movie!"

"I don't care about a goddamn movie!" I roared. "Can't you see I'm having a crisis here?"

"But...why?" he asked, bewildered.

"Because you're right! Here I am calling her hypercritical, but all I ever do is belittle her, mock her, argue with her!"

"Fay," Neil murmured, trying to talk me down.

"I do everything in my power," I continued, on a roll, "to be just the opposite of her! She only got a job because she had to; I wanted to have a career. She was overbearing with her kids; I'm...*laissez faire* with my own. She's cheap; I over-tip. She lies about her age; I let my hair go gray. I'm trying to be the anti-Sophie!"

"Will you just calm down?" Neil coaxed, as we made our way to the car amid the stares of the cinema staff.

"What's even worse is how I undermine her to her own granddaughter!" I suddenly realized. "She's the butt of the jokes I tell Olivia, about my mother's stinginess, her funny way of pronouncing words, her crazy worrying, her dieting, her love affair with bling. Whenever I mention my mother to her, it's to make fun of her. To put her down." I looked at him in horror. "Oh my God, Neil. What am I teaching her?"

"Come on, Fay," he soothed as he helped me into the

car. "Simmer down, now."

"I'm teaching her to be like me," I realized, answering my own question. "To move away from me, to put up walls between us. God, Neil! I'm a walking Harry Chapin song!"

I now saw my daughter's unreachability—by phone and also in person—as a continuation, a consequence of the emotional barriers I myself erected against my own mother. I viewed my mother as my enemy, as someone who did not accept me, but it was also true the other way around, that I was against her. I took Preet's side against her automatically, for instance, though it is perfectly possible that he is indeed stealing from her. Didn't one of Olivia's friends steal one of Olivia's dresses and swear it was hers? Didn't my friend Adrienne's cleaning lady steal one of her blouses (and then, like a putz, pose with it on Instagram)? Why did I take a stranger's word over my own mother's?

I grabbed Neil's lapel before he could start the car, so that I could look him in the eye.

"Is it me? Am I really a bad daughter?"

Neil's eyes were full of affection. "No, Fay. No way. You're a wonderful daughter, and a terrific mother. You have the patience of a saint sometimes. I never said your mom was an angel."

I wiped my eyes with my sleeve. "No. No, she's not," I agreed. "I may not be the perfect daughter, but she is definitely not the perfect mom."

"I never said she was, baby. Come on. I think we could both use a drink."

"Yeah," I laughed. "Now you're talkin'. Jaegermeister?"

"Whoa, there, slugger. I said a drink, not 'let's get shit-faced.'"

"Right. You have to drive. Wine, then," I proposed.

He grinned. "Yeah. Let's see if we can find a glass of wine in this city that doesn't cost a week's salary."

On the way back to the hotel, however, the wine marinating my brain, I went back to stewing. I felt like I was between a rock and a hard place, slowly being crushed. Like I was peanut butter and jelly squished in between two slices of crusty bread, a formless mess. I always had a bad relationship with my mother, I knew, but now I was realizing that the same might be true with Olivia, who seemed to put us—me—on the back burner of her life. Ah, Olivia. I both missed her and was furious with her. And somehow with myself. Maybe my husband and my mother were right. Maybe this was all my doing. Maybe I did let my daughter get away with murder. Should I have raised her differently? I suppose. But could I have raised her differently? The more I thought about it, the more I felt that no, I couldn't have. Not really. Because one thing I knew for sure was that I could never have brought up my daughter—*would* never have brought up my daughter—the way my mother had brought me up. Yes, I had to admit, it was true: I was angry with Sophie, and yes, I probably was not a very good daughter to her. But the reason for that was because she had not been a good mother to me. There. I've said it.

I know she put food on the table and clothes on our backs, as she repeated relentlessly whenever Gabe or I dared to complain as kids, but that does not a good mother make. A good mother reads to her kid, but I was the one who had to read to Gabe when we were little. A good mother takes her kid to the park, or to the kid's friend's house, not to watch said mother play gin rummy with her friends, expecting, no, *demanding* that her kids play with her friends' boring offspring. A good mother prepares food the kid likes, not food only she likes. If I even just smell cabbage soup I want to throw up. And a good mother doesn't teach her daughter to ride a bike by telling her any idiot can do it, and then when that daughter falls and cries, doesn't tell her there are worse pains in life, to stop exaggerating.

We entered our hotel room just as my phone rang. Of course, my mother. I let it ring. Neil, who had shot into the bathroom, emerged a few minutes later.

"Who was that? Didn't your phone ring?"

"It's late and I'm too tired to talk."

Neil eyed me. "You're too tired? Or you didn't want to answer it?"

"Both."

"Let me guess who it was: your mother." It didn't take a rocket scientist.

"I'm just too tired to deal with her now, Neil."

"You're going to have to deal with her sometime."

"Well, I can just imagine what she'll say when I tell her Olivia ditched us our entire trip."

"You know, Fay, it's really funny how you're this smart, accomplished adult woman, and yet when it comes to your mother, you cower as if you were a little kid."

"Thanks, honey. I really need this now," I said, dropping into the ugly beige chair.

"See? When it comes to me, you have no trouble saying what you think. You have no problem confronting me. But when it comes to your mother and frankly even your daughter, you just turn into jello."

"It's just such an effort, always having to do battle with my mother," I explained. "If I said the cat was black, no, it was dark gray. If I said that's a small dog, no, she'd say, it was a medium dog because her neighbor's dog, which is a toy poodle, now that's a small dog, and a German Shepherd, that's a big dog. She always has to be right. And more importantly, I have to be wrong."

"So why are you telling all this to me?" Neil asked. "Tell it to her."

"I can't."

"Why not?"

"Because it's impossible to talk to her."

"Come on, Fay."

I rested my head on my hand, and looked at Neil through splayed fingers without answering.

He wouldn't let up. "I mean, what do you think is going to happen if you stand up to her, to both of them?"

"I don't know," I mumbled. "I guess I'm afraid they won't...I don't know."

"They won't what?" he pressed.

"They won't..." I shook my head. I myself didn't know what I was saying.

"They won't what?" he persisted.

"You know...love me."

We were both silent for a moment. Even I was surprised.

"Won't love you?" Neil repeated, equally surprised. "You think if you say no to Olivia, she won't love you?" he asked, his voice implying the absurdity of the proposition.

"No. I just...don't want her to feel about me the way I feel about my mother."

"And how is that?" he pursued.

"I don't know," I hedged. "Angry. Like you said."

"About?"

"About how she always made me feel stupid and like a big disappointment in her life, with her harsh words and her criticisms. Even now that we are both adults, she always has something to criticize."

"So what?" he challenged. "Sometimes I criticize you, and you don't fall apart."

"You might criticize something I've done," I responded, "but not who I am."

"Come on," he protested. "She doesn't criticize who you are."

"Yeah she does, Neil. Yeah, she does."

"Come on," he repeated. "That's just her way, I guess."

"Yeah, that's her way, all right. That's her way of telling me I'm not good enough. That's her way of saying she…"

"She what?" he prodded when I didn't finish.

I just shook my head.

"She what?" he asked again.

"She just doesn't really…love me," I blurted, once more surprising myself.

Neil opened his eyes wide. "Wow. Really? You really think your mother doesn't love you, Fay?"

"Oh, I don't know what I think," I replied, frustrated. "It's just…mothers are supposed to love their children unconditionally. That's what I mean. I never felt that I was loved unconditionally."

And as if on cue, my phone rang.

"Babe," he said, putting his hands on my shoulders, "just talk to her."

With this, he absconded yet again to the bathroom, this time with the manual of one of the gadgets he'd just purchased. It was nice and thick. He'd have plenty of reading material to weather out the storm. I picked up my phone and answered.

"Hi Mom," I sighed.

"Hi!" she chirped. "How's it going?"

"Good. Good."

She got right to the point: "So how's our little girl?"

"Our little girl?" I laughed scornfully. "I have no idea."

"Huh? I don't understand."

I then proceeded to tell my mother about the whole trip's worth of not seeing Olivia.

"Oh my God, Fay! Oh my God!" My mother was practically speechless.

"Yeah," was all I could respond.

"Well, that is incredibly rude," she concluded. "You went all the way out there..."

"Yeah."

"You know I love that girl, but..."

"Yeah."

"I mean, if you had ever done anything like that to me..."

"Yeah, I know, Mom," I finally responded. "If I had ever done anything like that, you would have given me hell."

"Well, who wouldn't? Who does such a thing?"

I didn't answer.

"So what are you going to do?"

"Do?" I asked. "What do you mean? What can I do? We leave tomorrow. The trip is over."

"Well, but you're the parents."

"So? What does that mean?"

"I mean," she stammered, "you're just going to let her get away with this?"

"Um, what do you mean?" I began. "You mean, are we going to punish her?"

"Well, Fay, she shouldn't just be able to get away with something like this!"

I let out a breath I had apparently been holding. She continued.

"See? This is what I always tell you. You let that girl walk all over you. And this is what happens!"

"You know, Mom," I began, acidly, "maybe you're right.

Maybe I do let her get away with too much."

"That's right," she agreed, probably surprised at my words.

"But you know why? You want to know why?" I panted. "Because I didn't want to be like you."

She paused. "What?"

"I can see that how I've raised her hasn't been the ideal way of raising a child, I can see that now," I said, warming up, "but I swore I wouldn't raise Olivia to think she was stupid, to feel like a loser, a disappointment..."

"What?" my mother raised her voice. "What are you trying to say?"

"You know what I'm trying to say! All my life you've made me feel bad, criticized every little thing I did."

"No I didn't!"

"Yes, Mom, you did."

"Like when?" she challenged.

"Oh my God, where do I begin?" I laughed. "'I think we'll need to start shopping in the adult clothing section, 'cause my daughter loves Oreos too much ha ha!' Remember saying that to the saleslady at Macy's?"

"I never said that."

"You did. When we were shopping for a bathing suit, no less. I was twelve! How do you think that made me feel?"

"I'm sure I was just kidding. Don't be so sensitive."

"Right! I'm too sensitive! When I found out the girls in my class had a party and I was the only one they didn't invite, I cried and you told me I was being too sensitive!"

"So now everything is my fault?"

"You know what? Yeah! If you hadn't always criticized me, if you had only..." My voice trailed off when I realized what I was going to say.

"Only what?" she spat.

"Only...made me feel loved," I squeaked, my face burning.

She was silent for a moment. "What are you talking about? You're my daughter!"

As if that explained everything. I didn't answer.

"For God's sake, Fay! I know I'm not as…mushy as you wished I were. I know I'm a bit…tough. But I had to be! I was raising you and your brother on my own!"

"How does that prevent you from showing a little affection?" I demanded.

"Oh honestly…" she began, irritation in her tone. "Look. All I know is it's a hard world out there. I didn't want to raise kids who would crumble whenever anyone said something mean to them," she explained, elongating the word "mean" in mockery. "Those girls who didn't invite you to their party," she referred back, "I wanted you to learn how to deal with things like that. Not to give them the satisfaction of seeing you cry. To build you up."

"But I wasn't crying in front of them," I exploded. "I was crying in front of you! I was crying to my mother! Isn't that, like, the person you're supposed to cry to?"

She sighed in exasperation. "Really! Why are we dredging up these old things from the past? Why can't you ever let anything go?"

"Because these old things are what made me what I am today. A woman who wonders if her mother loves her. And a woman who doesn't say boo to her own daughter because she doesn't want her to feel like she always felt."

"So I'm a terrible mother, is that what you're trying to say?" she hurled at me.

I didn't know what to answer.

"Fay," she continued, softening her voice, "whatever you think of me, and maybe some of what you're saying might have some truth to it," and here her voice started to crack, "but whatever else you think, I have always…" Now her voice trailed off. God. She couldn't even say she loved me.

My own mother. "Maybe I don't always show it," she admitted. "Maybe I'm not good at showing it. But you know how I feel about you, Fay."

"Really? Does it sound like I know how you feel about me, Mom? Is that what you've been hearing from me?"

"Oh, honestly!" she exhaled. "Fine. I love you. There. Happy?"

"No, I'm not happy. It's like pulling teeth. It's like you said it out of—"

"If I don't say it you're mad, and if I do say it, you're still mad!" she griped. "I can't win!"

"You just don't sound like you mean it!"

"Well, maybe I'm not so good at saying it, but I do mean it," she said, in a calmer voice. "I do."

I remained silent. I didn't know what to do with this avowal of my mother's. Or even if I really believed her.

"If I criticize," she had to go on, "it's because I care. It's because I want to correct you, for you to be better—"

"Because the way I am isn't good enough?"

"You're twisting my words!"

"You know, Mom, there's such a thing as unconditional love, where you love someone no matter what. No matter what stupid thing they've done or said. That's how a mom should love her kid."

"Well, of course I do."

"No, Mom. I always felt you loved me only if. Only if I fulfilled certain conditions."

"Oh, honestly. Like what?"

"Like as long as I behaved a certain way, did as I was told, did what you wanted—"

"Really, Fay!" she cried.

"As long as I looked a certain way!" I pursued. "God forbid I should get fat! You were always going on about my weight, now my hair..."

"Are we going to go over this again? I told you why I comment on your hair…"

"And my weight?"

"Your weight is fine!"

"Now it's fine? Yet whenever I eat a chocolate or an ice cream, you start on me—"

"I'm just looking out for your health."

"No, Mom, not my health. My looks. Remember what you said to me after I had Olivia? That when you saw me at the end of my pregnancy you were shocked. That's the word you used. Shocked."

"Well, you were huge! Much bigger than was, you know, usual. And I only meant I was surprised."

"No, you meant you disapproved."

"So? Do I have to approve everything you do? Like you do with Olivia? And how's that working out for you?"

Oh, touché, Mom. It was like she had sucker-punched me. All the air had gone out of me. I realized I was exhausted. By everything. Her, Olivia. Me.

"Okay look, Mom," I sighed. "It's late and tomorrow we'll be back home. Can we continue this tomorrow?"

"Yeah, fine," she said. "We'll talk tomorrow."

"Okay, bye then."

"Bye. And Fay?"

"Mm hmm?"

"I'm…glad you're coming back. I've…missed you."

I smiled despite myself. I knew how hard it must have been for her to admit that.

"I've missed you too, Mom." Okay. A white lie.

Day Seven: **Last Day**

ME
Hi! We're just about to leave the hotel to pick you up. Be ready!

No answer, and no little check by our message. Was her phone turned off? Oh no.

"Let's just go there," Neil decided.

"You think? Should we just drive on over there?" I asked him, unconvinced. "What if she's not there?"

"So what do you suggest?" he snapped. "Just stay here in the room?"

"No, you're right. Worse comes to worst, we can do some more sightseeing."

The look he gave me belied that thought. "I swear, if she's not there…"

"Well, she has to be there," I assured him, and myself. "After all, we're getting on a plane today!"

On the way to Olivia's place, however, we finally received a text.

OLIVIA
Hi Mom! Sorry! My phone died

ME

Hi! We're on our way!

OLIVIA

Wait! I'm not home!

ME

What?? Where are you?

OLIVIA

We went to a club after the show, and then saw the sunrise and then crashed on a friend's floor!

"A club?!" Neil exclaimed. "How can she get into a club? She's nineteen!"

"No idea."

"Don't tell me she has a fake ID."

"Maybe it's one of those alcohol-free clubs," I offered.

He looked at me like I was certifiable.

"They do exist!" I protested.

"Who would go there? And why?"

"Under twenty-ones. And to dance," I answered.

"No one goes to clubs to dance," he declared. "People go to drink and to pick someone up." When the ramifications of his statement hit him, he paled. "Where did she say she spent the night?"

I sighed. This was why I left him in the dark about Olivia's birth control pills.

"'A friend,' she only said."

"Which friend? Male? Female?"

"Is this really the moment to go into all that? We have a plane to catch!"

"Right. Right." Neil shook the horrid images from his brain. "Tell her to meet us in her apartment. Tell her we're on our way."

ME

We're on our way to your apt. Meet us there.

OLIVIA

Can't we meet a bit laaaater? Pleeeeease?

I read her question aloud and received the expected vituperative response.

ME

Daddy says no.

OLIVIA

But it's my laaaaast day!!!!

ME

Daddy says no.

OLIVIA

Fine. Meet you there

But fifteen minutes later, we received another text.

OLIVIA

Mom, you're gonna have to give me some more time!

ME

Why?

OLIVIA

I can't find my keys

ME

What?!

OLIVIA

I must have left them at Rick's. So I have to go
back to get them
(Rick. Neil's nightmare come true.)

ME

We'll give you a lift.

OLIVIA

I'm already on my way there

ME

Fine. We'll wait outside your place.

But of course we couldn't wait outside her place. How
had we forgotten the purgatory of trawling for a parking
space? So we drove around a bit in circles, and finally decided
to park in a parking garage.

ME

Well? Where are you?

OLIVIA

Bad news. Looked everywhere for my keys but
they're not here!

Me

Oh my God Livy!

OLIVIA

On my way to the club from yesterday. Must have

lost them there. I'm gonna see if someone found them

ME

Is the club even open now?

OLIVIA

I'll let u know

"We're going to miss the plane!" Neil shouted.

"We're not going to miss the plane," I reassured him. "We've still got plenty of time."

"Tell her to call a locksmith."

"Yeah, great. She just moves in to a new apartment and then has a locksmith break the lock. The landlord's going to love her."

"Okay, okay," Neil conceded. "What about her roommates? Where are they?"

ME

What about your roommates?

OLIVIA

They're not with me

ME

Where are they?

OLIVIA

Stephanie's at her boyfriend's and not answering. Rachel idk

ME

So go to her boyfriend's if you don't find the keys

at the club.

OLIVIA

Idk where he lives

ME

You're kidding

OLIVIA

Not

ME

How can you not know where your best friend's boyfriend lives?!

OLIVIA

He's her boyfriend not mine!!!

ME

But haven't you ever been to his place? You said you went to a party there!

OLIVIA

Yeah but I can't remember where it is. It was night. I just went with Steph and Rachel

ME

It was night?? What does that mean?! Too dark to see where you're going? Too dark to read a street sign or a building number?!

OLIVIA

Mom!!!! I'm already so freaked out about this without you giving me more grief!!!!!

ME

I wish you could hear the grief Daddy's giving me.

OLIVIA

I'm soooo sorry!!!

ME

We'll deal with this later. Why don't you just call the landlord? You do have his number, don't you?

OLIVIA

Of course mom! I'm not a complete idiot

ME

So? Call him!

OLIVIA

He lives in Berkeley. That's like an hour away. It's quicker to try the club

ME

Fine. Let us know.

But an hour later, still nothing. Neil was pacing in front of Olivia's building like a caged panther at a zoo. Olivia had not answered the phone nor responded to my first five inquiries regarding her luck at the club. Finally, after my sixth text...

OLIVIA

Sorry Mom! The club was closed like you said. But I managed to get a hold of a friend who knows Chris and thinks he knows where he lives. So I'm on my way there

ME
He thinks he knows?

OLIVIA
He said he was there once and was pretty drunk
so we're going to try to find it while I keep trying
Steph

"They're going to *try* to find the boyfriend's apartment in all of San Francisco?!" Neil was beside himself.

"Of course they're not going to look in *all* of San Francisco," I retorted, losing my cool as well. Time was ticking away and we still had to go back to the hotel to pick up our stuff, which we hadn't wanted to leave in the trunk while we had lunch with Olivia. "He must know more or less where, for God's sake," I tried to convince the both of us.

ME
He knows more or less where, right?

OLIVIA
Yeah

ME
Like at least the street, right?

OLIVIA
He says yes. Pretty sure
(Pretty sure. My God.)

ME
Look, Olivia, why don't you just get a locksmith?
How much could that cost?

OLIVIA
Mom let me just try this first!!!

Her exclamation points seemed to reprimand me, as if I were the one who had caused all this mess. But I wasn't about to get snippy now.

ME
Fine. Let us know. We're going to find a place to eat.

We ate in a diner that charged twenty dollars for a burger. The day was getting better and better. We split the fries. After another hour and multiple prompts, Olivia restored communication.

OLIVIA
Well, we found Chris's place

ME
And?

OLIVIA
They're not there

ME
Where are they?

OLIVIA
His roommate doesn't know. Said they left an hour ago

ME
Time to get a locksmith

OLIVIA

I guess

ME

Do it

OLIVIA

Fine

ME

You know what? Never mind. Daddy and I will get one. Meet us here

After calling a few locksmiths in the general vicinity, we found one who was actually available. Who knew so many people got locked out on a daily basis? But when we explained our predicament, we came upon an obstacle.

"So you say it's your daughter's apartment?"

"Yes. And she's locked out."

"Where is she?"

"She's on her way."

"Wait. She's not with you?"

"Like I said, she's on her way."

"Uh, you know, I can't let you in. I can only let the tenant in," he explained.

"She'll be here! She's on her way!" I assured him.

"I can't do anything till she's there."

"So...what? You can't even get here in the meantime?"

"How long is she gonna be?" he asked.

How should I know? "Soon!"

"Look, it'll only take me fifteen, twenty minutes tops to get there. Call me when she's almost there, okay?"

It was worse than trying to get a doctor to make a house call. Three quarters of an hour later, Olivia texted her imminent arrival. We frantically punched in the locksmith's number. But we were in for another surprise.

"Okay," he answered. "I'm on my way."

"Great!"

"But one more thing I forgot to mention."

"Yeah? What's that?"

"I gotta see some proof of residence."

"Proof of residence?" I squeaked. "Like what?"

"Anything. Gas bill, electric bill…"

"She just moved in! She hasn't paid any bills yet!"

"So the rental contract."

"Okay. Okay. We'll tell her." But I already had a bad feeling about this.

ME

Liv, have you got your rental contract?

OLIVIA

Of course I do! What kind of a doof do you think I am??

(Neil strangled a response.)

ME

Good. Bring it.

OLIVIA

Oh what? You mean with me?

ME

Yes

OLIVIA

I don't have it!

ME

Well where is it?

(But of course I already knew the answer.)

OLIVIA

In the apartment!!!

ME

Call the landlord!

OLIVIA

All right already!!!

By this point, we were cutting it close on time. We didn't want to take the chance that we'd hit traffic on the way back to the hotel or that some other mishap might occur, so we abandoned our perch in front of Olivia's building and headed back to our hotel.

ME

We'll pick you up on our way to the airport

OLIVIA

Ok thx

But on our way to Olivia's:

OLIVIA

Mom! I had an emergency! I'm not at my apartment!

ME

What?! What emergency?!

OLIVIA

Our friend's dog that we were dog sitting for a few days got sick! He started puking and wouldn't stop! I had to take him to the vet!

ME

You?! What about Stephanie and Rachel?!

OLIVIA

They weren't here!

ME

Olivia!!!! We have a plane to catch!

OLIVIA

Don't worry. Rachel is on her way. As soon as she gets here I'm going!

ME

When will that be?

OLIVIA

Look, why don't you guys go straight to the airport and I'll meet you there?

ME

Olivia you are really cutting it close!

OLIVIA

Don't worry! I'll be there!

ME

Daddy says don't you dare miss this flight!

OLIVIA

I won't! Promisssssse!

But she wasn't at the airport.

ME

Hi. We're at the airport.

ME

Where are you?

ME

Olivia!

"She's not answering." Neil, who had been trying to call her on his phone, summed up the situation. "Can you believe it? She's not answering!"

I remained silent, fretting. I wasn't about to defend Olivia now. "Try again," I suggested.

"This is the fourth time I've called, Fay! What do you think I'm doing?" he shouted. People turned to look at us.

"You don't have to yell at me," I whispered loudly.

"What do you want from my life?" he groused. "I just want to strangle her."

"I know, I know. I'm sure she'll come. I'm sure she's on her way."

"Then why the hell isn't she answering her phone?"

"I really don't know," I admitted. "But I'm sure she'll come."

"Oh really?" he challenged. "What makes you so sure?"

"Oh, come on, Neil. She's not going to miss her flight!"

"How do you know?"

"Because...come on." I looked at him in wonder. "No one misses their flight."

"Yeah, Fay, lots of people miss their flights. People who don't give a shit. People who didn't pay for their tickets."

"Stop it, Neil. I know she's flighty, but even Olivia wouldn't do that."

"Then why isn't she here?"

"I'm sure she's on her way. Call her again."

In the meantime, I kept frantically texting her.

ME
Olivia, they're going to start boarding soon!

ME
They've started boarding!

ME
Our group is supposed to board next!! Where are you??

ME
They're calling last boarding call!

ME
Olivia!!

Finally we boarded our plane. Even while we were in our seats I texted, and when they told us to put our phones in airplane mode, I still thought I'd see her rushing through the door at the last minute. Even when they announced that the cabin doors were closed and we were ready for take-off, I almost believed the doors would burst open and Olivia would swoosh in, all frazzled and breathless from running to catch the plane. Like in a movie. But she didn't, and we took off without her. Without my baby.

When we landed in Houston, on our stopover, we saw the messages from Olivia.

OLIVIA

I'm sooooo sorry guys, really

OLIVIA

It was just one screw-up after another. I couldn't help it. I'm really soooo sorrrrry!!!

"No, it was you screwing up, one after another!" Neil shouted, as if she could hear. We didn't even call her, that's how angry we were. We couldn't trust ourselves not to shout in front of the whole airport.

ME

We are beside ourselves with anger, Olivia.

OLIVIA

I said I was sorry
(As if that made everything okay.)

ME

You missed your flight! We paid for that ticket!

OLIVIA

It's ok! Like I said I changed the ticket! No prob!

ME

For when?

OLIVIA

For Xmas!

"Christmas!" Neil whacked his hand against his forehead. "We came out all that way for nothing!"

I was speechless. And textless. At first.

> ME
>
> Listen to me, Olivia. You think your behavior was acceptable? Do you really think it's all OK, just because you changed the ticket? You ditched us for your friends, and even for your friends' parents! You made us come all the way out there, only to not see you, not even once! And then you don't even have the decency to show up at the airport??

> OLIVIA
>
> Mom! Don't make me feel bad!!!

> ME
>
> Are you kidding?? Of course you should feel bad! You let us down, Olivia. You treated us badly. This is really unforgivable.

Neil, to whom I had been reading aloud my text, looked at me with grim approval. "Fay, you're finally acting like... like a parent."

> OLIVIA
>
> Mom!!!

> ME
>
> Don't Mom me! And since you're staying there, you'd better get yourself a job! If you're old enough to make your own travel plans, and go to bars, you're old enough to take care of yourself.

OLIVIA

I will!

ME

Fine. We'll speak when we get to NJ.

Whereupon I turned my phone off. I did not want to hear one more excuse from her. Neil, too, was fuming.

"Next time you want to visit our daughter," he joked, "we're going to Vegas instead."

"Might as well," I agreed. "No point visiting someone who wants you out of her life. The girl is gone, just like that."

Neil put his arm around me, seeing how hurt I was. "She's not gone forever. She'll be home for Christmas, she said."

"No, Neil, you were right. She's leaving. Sure, she'll come back now and then, but this is the beginning of the end. She's on her way out. Her life is away from us. And I just have to accept that."

I suddenly recalled the homeless guy, hanging on to our car, risking it dragging him under its wheels. Oh my God, that was me, I realized. I was the one who didn't know when to let go, who harmed myself and those around me by holding on. I was being dragged under by my own desperation, by my suffocating need. Yes, some things you have to hold on to in life. But some things you need to let go.

I sat there, close to tears, brooding on Olivia, on me, on us. Suddenly I turned my phone back on and began typing furiously.

ME

You know, Olivia, we are human beings! We have feelings! I have feelings! I am a person, not just something to make your life easier, not just someone to run your errands and pay your bills. Not just someone to listen to your problems. I have problems too! I exist!

Then I turned my phone off and kept it off.

We hardly spoke on our drive back home from the airport. We were tired, but it was more than that. We were sick and tired. Once inside the house, however, everything seemed ever so quiet. I, frankly, was miserable.

And once again, I had barely set my foot inside the threshold when my mother called. It's like she had a tracer on my phone.

"Hi!" she gushed. "So how's our California Girl?"

"Our California Girl is fine!" I snorted. "And she's still in California."

"What? What happened? Did she miss the flight?"

I was about to answer yes, when I realized that Olivia didn't actually miss her flight because she had already changed her ticket. Had already decided she didn't want to come back with us. And hadn't cared what we would say, what we would think. She made her decision according to her own whims. Which was something I was going to need to start learning to do.

"Oh," my mother said after I explained it to her. "I'm so disappointed."

"Imagine how I feel."

"I guess you're pretty angry," she allowed.

I sighed. "Actually, to be honest, I'm not only angry. I'm also a bit sad."

"Yeah, I get it," she said, not really getting it at all. "When your kid leaves home, it's tough."

I had meant that I was sad about my own failure as a mother, and about Olivia's failing my expectations of her as a daughter. I was sad that I had held illusions—delusions—about our relationship, sad that Olivia had seen me as an easy mom, an enabling mom, and not truly as a friend. I was sad that indeed I had been that enabler, that wannabe friend, when I suppose I should have been her mother.

"Yeah," I agreed, deciding to go with it. "At least you had Gabe still at home after I left."

"Yes, but Gabe is Gabe and you are you. It was still hard. When your daughter leaves home, it's like you've lost your best friend."

"Mmm."

"Well, not *like*. It *was* my best friend leaving, since you're my best friend."

"I'm your best friend?" I croaked, shocked.

"Of course you are! Who else?"

"Oh, I don't know. Mona?"

"Mona? Come on. Of course *nottttte*."

"Aunt Deirdre?" I suggested.

She clicked her tongue in impatience. "She's my sister." As if that explained everything. "Of course you're my best friend. Who else do I tell all my secrets to?"

"Uh, no one!" I cackled. "No one knows your secrets!"

She laughed, too. "Well, there's that. But I feel like I can talk to you. Like I can trust you with my, you know, thoughts and feelings."

This was momentous! My mother was actually talking about thoughts and feelings. With me! But God, I felt so guilty! I was the last person she could trust her thoughts and feelings with, since they were the fodder of all my jokes and ridicule. I was the worst friend in the world! The worst daughter!

"Well," I gulped, and added noncommittally, "I'm glad you feel that way, Mom."

"I do. And I hope you feel that way about me. That you can tell me anything."

So much for non-commitment. But really, had she not heard a word I had said to her the day before? This was the entire crux of my problem with her: that I did not feel I could open up to her, that I did not trust her with my feelings. Or had she indeed heard me, and was trying to make a gesture, trying to respond? Was my mother trying to become my friend?

I thought again about Olivia, how I had prided myself on her willingness to open up to me, and realized I had been smugly comparing our relationship to the one between me and my mother. I had allowed myself to believe that ours—mine and Olivia's—was superior because of me, because I was a better mother. But perhaps it was because of Olivia. Perhaps if Olivia had closed herself off, as I have with my mother, our relationship would indeed be like my mother's and mine. I had always wanted to be different from my mother, including being a different kind of mother. But was I necessarily a better mother? Hardly. Was my relationship with Olivia all that ideal? Hadn't I raised an irresponsible, selfish child? Didn't I pander to her every need and excuse her every fault? And look at the role model I had been. Olivia saw how I lied to my mother, hid from my mother, derided her, dismissed her. Is that how she would grow to treat me? Isn't that how she was treating me already?

My own grandmother used to tell us a story called "The Wooden Bowl." In it, a family was coming to grips with their grandmother's aging. She began getting confused about money so they took her wallet. She began forgetting where she lived so they locked her in the house. She began wetting the bed so they made her sleep on the patio. She began dropping her dishes so they made her eat out of a wooden bowl (I guess this was before plastic). One day, the grandmother's daughter saw her own son in the garden working on some handicraft.

"What are you doing, my boy?" she asked him.

"I'm making a wooden bowl."

"A wooden bowl," she repeated, surprised. "What for?"

"Why, for you and Dad," he responded. "For when you get old, like Grandma."

Is Olivia preparing my wooden bowl? And should I be surprised if she does?

And as for my mother, does she even merit all this attitude from me? I remembered her saying, "Why can't you ever let anything go?" It was true. I held on to my anger; I held on to my pain. But why? Was she really such a bad mother? Is anyone really a perfect parent? I obviously wasn't. Nor was I a good daughter. I made fun of my mother's vanity, for instance, but not my own. Though I allowed my hair to remain gray, I can't say I viewed it without fear, not just the fear of aging and the fear of death, but also the banal fear of being ugly. Why, then, could I not accept my mother's concern for her appearance?

After all, we are all afraid, and sometimes our fears are not base and selfish but are born of love. I recall the time Olivia came with me to my yoga class. I had been going for three years and Olivia, at her first class, was able to do a headstand and a handstand. I had chalked it up to a young and limber body. But the instructor had explained that Olivia was able to do these challenging poses because she lacked fear. She told us she noticed that after they had children, her students were less daring with the more gravity-defying positions, suddenly afraid they would fall or hurt themselves, even if they had been able to do handstands or whatever before. She surmised that on an unconscious level they realized someone now depended on them, and therefore they could not afford to get hurt. They now had a new fear.

I recalled the time I witnessed a robbery at gunpoint in my gym. I had dropped Olivia off at a birthday party so I had some time to myself. I was on a stationary bike on the second floor, when there was shouting and then shots fired. We all ran for cover, expecting the gunman to come up the stairs at any moment and pick us off, one by one. As I crouched behind one of the machines, my heart thudding and convinced I was about to die, only one thought crowded my mind, only one name was on my lips: Olivia, Olivia, Olivia. All I could think was, "What will become of Olivia?" That was my fear. A fear, moreover, that never diminishes.

Why isn't she answering her phone? Where are they at this hour? What is that weird rash on her back?

And we fear for ourselves, too. Having kids makes you keenly aware of the passage of time. You blink and they're in kindergarten. Blink again, they're off to college. Yet while this passage of time means they are blooming, ripening, for us, their parents, it means we are fading, decaying. Dying. My mother, for instance, has become ever more fearful for her health over the years, more preoccupied with taking care of herself, almost to the point of neurosis. Hence the sweaters. I laugh, but she worries about getting sick and dying because she is indeed creeping closer to death. We are all marching toward the Grim Reaper, but my mother is nearly ringing his doorbell.

Why, then, could I not see her reluctance to reveal her age as a reflection of her own fears, especially those of aging and death? Why did I take my own fears seriously, but not hers? I made fun of her when she claimed her wrinkles were from stress and not old age, yet what about my own vanity? Did I hate to wear my glasses in public because I thought they made me look ugly? Or because they made me look old? Why could I accept my own fears but not hers?

Why did I only think of my own bereavement at my father's death, and not sympathize with hers, not recognize her despair at being left alone and, with my father's death, being reminded of her own ever-imminent end?

Maybe I don't feel the same nearness of death, but I do understand loss. Walking through my house now and seeing old photos, the ghosts of Olivia-at-age-nine, of toddler-Olivia, forced me to reckon with the sense that the Olivia-that-was is no longer the Olivia-that-is. Of course the passage of time saddens me, and the sense that all of us must die. But more to the point, what I mourn is rather the relationship that existed between us when she was a child, how Olivia was vis-à-vis myself. I reminisced about how she clung to me, trusted me, looked up to me. Loved me. When she was little and, ever questioning, used to respond to one of my statements with "How do you know?" I'd answer flippantly, "Because I know everything." One day, she asked me something and I casually threw out, "Oh, I don't know." She looked at me in shock. "You said you know everything!" I kind of thought she had gotten my little joke all along, but of course she was a little kid, and she hadn't. Of course she had taken me literally. With surprise I realized she had honestly believed I knew everything.

Imagine being so wise in someone else's eyes. Imagine being the source of everything honest and warm and good and true in someone else's eyes. I didn't appreciate that then, how she felt about me. I was always harried, stressed, hurrying from one thing to another. She was at times even a burden to me. I remember how I couldn't wait to put her into bed and finally be "free." I was always so tired. Well, I'm still tired and Olivia is a continent away. I'm free now. Free to hear the rooms echo with her absence, with my loneliness. I know I'm carrying on as if she were dead, God forbid, when she's only in California. But the pain is real. I have an Olivia-sized hole in my world, due to both physical and emotional distance. And nothing comes close to filling it.

Then Lulu died. A few days after we returned, she suddenly started wobbling instead of walking, and stopped eating. I took her to the vet and he gave her serum and blood transfusions, plus a ton of vitamins and probiotics that cost more than even Neil's precious trove, and when we brought her home she seemed better. But then again she stopped eating and hardly seemed able to walk. The X-rays showed she had cancers in various parts of her body. When she wouldn't even drink water, the vet said it was time.

I sobbed. I didn't cry; I sobbed. For Lulu, and for myself. First Olivia and now this. I called to tell Olivia, who also broke down in tears. After all, Lulu had been technically hers. We had gotten the dog for her as a birthday present when she turned ten, though obviously at ten she was more the nominal caretaker than the genuine one. I was the one who had fed her, walked her, taken her to the vet. But Olivia was the one who had named her, played with her and whose bed she had slept on.

"I wasn't there!" she wailed.

"No," I agreed. "But I was."

"But I wanted to be there with her!"

"I know, but at least she wasn't alone in the end." Or maybe being with me was the same as being alone, as I am a non-entity? In any event, as usual, Olivia only thought of herself. Maybe one day she would have a child and learn what it is to think of someone else, what it is to sacrifice, to sacrifice your hard-earned money, your sleep, your comfort, your very body, your enjoyment, your feelings. And if need be, your life.

My mother was more sympathetic to my grief than Olivia was, since my mother didn't have a personal interest. Indeed, she was not a dog person, and shuddered whenever

Lulu, hoping for a treat or at least a sign of affection, would approach her. And of course it was always to my mom, the one person who didn't want to cuddle, to put it mildly, to whom Lulu would come bounding over again and again, never taking the hint.

"Aw, geez, I'm so sorry for you," she said when I told her. "I know how much you were attached to her."

"Yeah, thanks Mom."

"Boy, first Olivia leaves and now the dog."

"Yeah, exactly," I said, a little surprised she had thought along the same lines as me.

"Are you going to get another one?"

"No. No one can replace Lulu," I said, my voice catching.

"But I guess you'll feel really lonely."

"I guess."

"Well, I'm here."

"Thanks, Mom."

"And I know what it's like to be lonely."

"I know, Mom."

"After your father died, it was very hard for me."

"I know, Mom."

"Of course, you can't compare a dog to a husband."

"Of course not."

"It was like my whole world crashed."

"I'm sure."

"So you'll get over this. If I could, you will."

"Right."

"You know what I was thinking about yesterday?" she prompted, changing the subject.

"No, what?"

"Remember that class trip of yours to see the opera *Carmen?*"

"Sure I do."

"They asked for chaperones and I volunteered. You were,

like, maybe ten years old. I had such a great time. You know I love the theater. So did your father, God rest his soul. And it was so nice to take you to your first opera."

I did remember. I, too, loved the theater, even at that age, for my parents had taken us to see one or two musicals on stage. I loved the whole ambience: the seats, the plush curtains, the printed programs, the hush as the lights went down. I thrilled to see the actors up close, to hear them sometimes flub their lines and laugh. I had never been to an opera, however, and all my schoolmates and I expected fat ladies in horned helmets shrieking in foreign tongues. Instead, though I couldn't understand the words, it was all crystal-clear to me how Carmen flirted, how Don José was jealous. I loved the music, the costumes.

But more than anything, it was one of my fondest memories of my mother. I remember being so proud of her, that the chaperone of our group was *my* mother. She had dressed up and I remember she was wearing a skirt suit and heels. I wanted to shout to everyone around me, "This is my mom!" And I remember her own excitement at being there, at the opera, with me. I remember her grabbing my hand and squeezing it as the curtain rose. Normally I would have died of embarrassment for anyone to see my mother hold my hand. But this time I intuited the gesture as born of her own excitement, which she was sharing with me, as an equal. As if we weren't mother and daughter, but rather friends.

"Yeah, I remember, Mom. I remember being so proud of you that day, that you were the chaperone."

"Really? We had a good time, didn't we? The two of us?"

"We did."

"We should do stuff more often, you and me."

"We should. You're right. We should."

"Especially now that Olivia's left, and Lulu. You're going to need the company."

"I guess."

"Well, you let me know."

Normally I would have left it at that. Normally I would never have even entertained the notion of doing something with my mom unless I actually had to. But suddenly I heard myself proposing, "Um…well, how about Saturday?"

She was silent for a moment, probably just as shocked as I was by my suggestion.

"We could grab lunch or go to the mall, I don't know," I pursued.

"Really? That sounds great! I'd love that! Sure! Saturday!"

I paused. I was already half-regretting my action. I feared it would be a disaster. Would we fight? Would she drive me crazy? And of course I felt guilty for even having these thoughts. Even her enthusiasm made me feel guilty. It shouldn't be such a big deal for your daughter to suggest spending time with you, should it?

I read an article once about the difference between guilt and shame. Guilt was feeling bad about an act; shame was feeling bad about yourself. I had been feeling shame that my mother thought I wasn't good enough, but maybe that wasn't true. She wanted to be with me. She appreciated me, it would seem, though maybe she didn't always agree with my choices and actions. She loved me, in her way. Yes, I felt guilty but maybe that could serve as a learning experience to do better, to make better choices. To be a better person. To be, perhaps, a better daughter?

Yes, I needed to be better. I couldn't keep focusing on loss, on absence. Olivia will grow up. One day she will come to appreciate us. And Neil is right; he's still here. And so is Sophie. And my friends. And me. I'm still here.

I realized that I had gotten it wrong about holding on versus letting go. They aren't mutually incompatible. They are two parts of a whole. It's only by knowing what to let go of, and when, that we manage to hold on to the things we love. To the people we love.

"Hello?" my mother asked, after I had let my pause lengthen. "Are you still there?"

"Yeah, Mom," I responded. "I am. I'm still here."

ACKNOWLEDGEMENTS

A few years ago, my husband, Jaime, and I flew to San Francisco to help our daughter, Claire, move out of her dorm, and the first day we were there, she couldn't see us because she had finals. This provided the kernel of *Texting Olivia,* thanks to Mark Schreiber, my friend and fellow author who, upon hearing my tale, said, "Wouldn't that make a funny story if the daughter didn't see the parents for their whole trip?" I said, "No, that's too silly," but a month later, I had the first draft written. So my first round of thanks goes to Mark Schreiber, for his idea, his encouragement and, primarily, his friendship. I'd also like to thank Lauren Grosskopf, my publisher, for taking on the project, and for her extreme dedication and tirelessness, despite my constant corrections and meddling. I'd like to thank as well my agent, Gail Hochman, for believing in me.

Special thanks to my two initial readers, Diana Rawlinson and Ruth Roman, beloved sister-in-law and friends (for Diana is both) whom I knew I could depend upon for an objective critique and whose wholehearted enthusiasm for the novel buoyed my own. I'd also like to thank Chris Clarke, Lenny Karpman, Gary Williams and Mike Crump, who read what would become excerpts of the book and cheered me on.

Finally and most importantly, my family. This novel could not have been written without the succor and faith of my husband, Jaime, my fellow traveler, in San Francisco and in life. I also thank my parents, who supported—financially and morally—a daughter who chose Creative Writing as her college major (but only because we all believed I was a pre-law student and therefore, I had told them, it didn't matter).

And I haven't forgotten Claire, along with her brothers, Isaiah and Jacob, who unwittingly provided much material for this book. Worried about comparisons between Olivia and Claire, I told my daughter, "I hope you don't think Olivia is you," to which she replied, "Mom, chill. No one cares but you."

GALYA GERSTMAN was born in New Jersey. She obtained her BA in Creative Writing at Barnard College and her PhD in French Literature from Columbia University in New York. She taught at Tel Aviv University before moving to Costa Rica to marry and begin a family and a writing career. She has published articles in academic journals and humorous essays in various online media. Her experience sending her kids off to college provided background and inspiration for *Texting Olivia*.